Dilma's Downfall

*The Impeachment of
Brazil's First Woman President
and the Pathway to Power
for Jair Bolsonaro's Far-Right*

By Peter Prengaman
and Mauricio Savarese

T0124567

The Associated Press
200 Liberty Street
New York, NY 10281
www.ap.org

"Dilma's Downfall" copyright © 2021 by Peter Prengaman
and Mauricio Savarese

All rights reserved.

No part of this work may be reproduced, or stored in a retrieval system,
or transmitted in any form or by any means, electronic, mechanical,
photocopying, recording, or otherwise, without express written permission
of the publisher.

Paperback: 978-1-7358459-9-9
(Published by The Associated Press, New York)
E-book: 978-1-7338462-9-5

Cover design by Deena Warner Design
Interior design by Kevin Callahan/BNGO Books
Project Oversight: Peter Costanzo

Visit AP Books: www.ap.org/books

Mauricio dedicates this book to all the Brazilians who inspired him to tell this story. He also dedicates it to his uncle Renato for being a courageous reporter and his mother, Meire, who worked as a maid and taught her three children that education matters. Finally, Mauricio dedicates it to his young daughter Carolina, who he hopes will cherish the core values of democracy and find books like this a reason to debate and propel the world forward.

Peter dedicates this book to wife Lorena and sons Tomás, Lucas and Pablo, who all sacrificed at times so Dad could write. He also dedicates it to younger brothers Charlie and Jamie, adopted as babies from Recife, Brazil. Initial trips to Brazil in 1985 and 1986, when Peter was 10 years old, inspired a life-long passion for the country that led to Portuguese study and eventually working as a journalist based in Rio de Janeiro.

Contents

Foreword

Dilma Rousseff, Brazil's former president, defies easy categorization.

Born affluent, she took up arms against Brazil's military dictatorship. An economist, she led the country from a period of economic plenty to a deep recession. And although she was head of state during years when a massive graft scheme was unearthed, threatening the top tiers of Brazil's political class and that of neighboring countries, she was never accused of corruption for personal gain.

But her story, with its complex turns, and the story of her impeachment in 2016, is also the story of modern Brazil.

Understanding how she came to be the country's first female president and why she was ousted from the position reveals much about how Brazil came to be where it is: torn by political divisions, mired in ongoing corruption scandals and trapped in an economic slump worsened by the pandemic.

Combining their personal experiences of covering the drama of Rousseff's impeachment with deep research and interviews, Mauricio Savarese and Peter Prengaman, former colleagues of mine at The Associated Press, have written a detailed examination of this critical period in Brazil's political history, producing an essential book for Brazil watchers and, more broadly, for watchers of democracy.

"Dilma's Downfall" captures the often larger-than-life personalities of the main players in the impeachment, such as Rousseff; her patron, former president Luiz Inácio Lula da Silva, himself an incredible story of transformation from union leader to president of Latin America's largest nation; and her nemesis, Eduardo Cunha, the Bible-verse-quoting speaker of the House and driving force for her removal.

The narrative also shows how the impeachment, and all its fallout, provided a clear opening for President Jair Bolsonaro and the hard right. Before Rousseff's removal, Bolsonaro was a fringe member of Congress, offering political observers little reason to believe he could mount a credible presidential campaign, much less win the nation's confidence.

But Brazil's overlapping political and economic crises — fueled by a downturn in commodity prices that deflated Brazil's prospects and headlines that blared near daily reminders of the unscrupulousness of the country's politicians — drove the population to fury with the status quo.

Many turned against Rousseff, who struggled to connect with voters. Bolsonaro seized the moment to animate his master narrative that the country had been led astray by the left, which had won the four previous elections.

When members of Congress lined up to cast their vote on her impeachment, Bolsonaro stood out by giving arguably his most memorable speech in his 27 years in the chamber: He dedicated his vote to the colonel who headed the intelligence and repression agency that detained Rousseff, and tortured her, during the dictatorship.

To Rousseff's supporters, her removal was a coup. To opponents, including many disenchanted Brazilians across the political spectrum, removing a president who had grown unpopular seemed a way to end gridlock in Congress and allow the battered financial sector to begin recovering. The country would get a fresh start with the 2018 presidential elections.

As Savarese and Prengaman show, her removal had lasting consequences for the nation. Democracy, which only returned to Brazil in the late 1980s, was under threat. Divisions were deepened, no small thing in a racially diverse country with a long history of inequality. And the process laid bare an underbelly of sexism and violent political rhetoric.

In sum, the nation did not emerge unscathed. In many ways, the fallout from impeachment is still being felt in 2021.

Juliana Barbassa
Latin America and Caribbean Editor
The New York Times

Introduction

Brazil today is far from the nation it was in 2010, when the economy was booming and millions were emerging from poverty. The Latin American powerhouse appeared then to be finally living up to the first part — and eliminating the second, sarcastic part — of the common phrase that it was "the country of the future and always will be."

Just over a decade later, Brazil is being led by President Jair Bolsonaro, a former Army captain who doesn't even try to hide the fact that he sees democracy as a dubious form of governing. The economy, not long ago a darling of emerging markets worldwide, has yet to fully recover from a recession that began in 2015. And political divisions, which became pronounced during 2013 protests and have festered ever since, are very deep, exacerbated by seemingly non-stop corruption scandals, by economic angst and, most recently, by the handling of the coronavirus crisis.

While the reasons for the decline are numerous, a nearly year-long saga in the middle of the decade, the 2015-2016 impeachment process and eventual ousting of President Dilma Rousseff, brought so many of Brazil's problems into view. Those problems were years in the making, but the way they came to the fore, in such a national, public way that deepened divisions, set the stage for large political and cultural shifts in the following years.

For example, seismic developments in Brazil in 2018, such as the rise of Jair Bolsonaro and the jailing of former President Luiz Inácio Lula da Silva, just to name a few, gained momentum during the impeachment process against Rousseff. Wanting to explain how today's Brazil came to be was one of the many reasons we decided to do a book focused on her impeachment.

Both of us, a Brazilian reporter who has long covered politics and an American editor and Brazil bureau chief for The Associated Press, were united in our astonishment that a democratically elected president could be ousted on such arguably flimsy accusations. We were also surprised that Rousseff, a trained economist who had worked closely with the charismatic Lula for years, had so many difficulties navigating Brazil's economy and political system, which ultimately led to her demise.

To say such things may sound naive, as any casual student of Latin America would note that Brazil's history is filled with volatile moments. Democracy only returned in 1985 after a 21-year military dictatorship. But in 2015, despite long-standing problems, Brazil was a major player on the world stage and one of the most stable nations in the Western Hemisphere. Its democracy had also withstood many major challenges that could have been much more potentially destabilizing than the overall situation in 2015. These included hyper-inflation in the 1990s and a mega corruption scandal in the early 2000s.

We were also motivated by this: While covering impeachment firsthand and then continuing to report on its fallout in subsequent years, it often felt that much confusion persisted about what actually transpired. Ask an average Brazilian what happened to Rousseff, and the answer could be almost anything: She and her Workers' Party were corrupt; she was a bad president; she bungled the economy; right-wing forces ousted her in a coup; or the country got tired of having a woman president. These were just a few of the more mainstream ideas (and there are many conspiracy theories). What you most likely wouldn't hear is any real discussion of the actual charges that led to her ouster.

That is not to say the impeachment process and aftermath were not covered by a robust and often opinionated Brazilian press and many foreign outlets, as they certainly were. But the day-to-day coverage did not always capture the full drama that played out. It was easy to miss many personalities and factors, some of them seemingly unrelated but connected in important ways, that contributed to this drama. There was the pressure of preparing simultaneously to host the Summer Olympics. There was a constant undercurrent of misogyny, both in the streets and in Congress, as Rousseff suffered verbal assaults and criticisms based on her gender. There were behind-the-scenes intrigues, rivalries and ambitions at play among Brazil's congressional leaders. There were macro political trends — exemplified by the progressivism that lifted Lula and, conversely, the strongman trend in many parts of the world that Bolsonaro reflected. There were betrayals and some comic factors — both of these embodied in a vice president who expressed himself in arcane Portuguese, had a decades-younger wife and a penchant for both poetry and whipping votes in congress.

Other key personalities included Rousseff's defeated presidential rival who had refused to accept the results of the 2014 election, fueled a growing political divide and accused Rousseff of corruption despite his own long list of mounting allegations. And there was the speaker of the lower chamber of Congress, dogged by numerous corruption allegations, who would lead the impeachment charge.

We have structured the narrative with those connections in mind. Focusing on the roughly nine-month period between when impeachment legislation was submitted and Rousseff was permanently removed, we introduce key events chronologically while detailing the backstories. Our hope is that this examination helps readers better understand what happened to Brazil and where the country may be headed. And whether those readers are in Brazil or elsewhere in a world in which many democracies are facing significant stress, we hope they may find cautionary lessons in our exploration of Dilma Rousseff's downfall. As we'll show, strong forces had long wanted Rousseff out. Impeachment simply turned out to be the vehicle that worked.

CHAPTER 1

The Stage Is Set

On the day that would mark the beginning of the end of her presidency, Brazilian President Dilma Vana Rousseff got up at 5:30 a.m. and prepared to go cycling. While she pedaled through the capital of Brasília, passing large modernist buildings and flanked by security, she reflected on a dream she had had recently.

Instead of feeling the heat from lawmakers, as she had since the beginning of her second term, in the dream the president was applauded in Congress. For an instant, she was happy despite more than a year of fighting that had gotten her and the country to this point. But that was not the reality.

Later that day — Wednesday, December 2, 2015 — impeachment proceedings were launched against Rousseff.

"She believed it would get it sorted out," said Carlos Araújo, her ex-husband and close friend. "She was ready to fight."

Brazil's first woman president strongly believed that reason would come to enemy politicians and businessmen, and that despite frustration over her handling of the economy, they would eventually back down. If that didn't happen, Rousseff and supporters boasted, the Supreme Federal Tribunal, the country's highest court, would block any impeachment effort. After all, they said her adversaries did not really have a case against her. "Fiscal maneuvering" was her supposed offense. Former presidents had done the same kind of budget moves she was accused of and faced no consequences. Rousseff was not facing allegations of corruption for personal gain, nor had she ever been.

She believed that growing street protests against her would subside by the end of December, when the Southern Hemisphere's summer begins and many Brazilians take vacations and spend time on the beach. That kind of a slow fade was what had happened to big demonstrations in 2013, the year before Brazil hosted the World Cup. And in August 2016, Rio de Janeiro would host the Olympic Games, which she and her mentor, former President Luiz Inácio Lula da Silva, had secured for the country in 2009, beating out U.S. President Barack Obama's Chicago and Tokyo and Madrid.

Although a tall order, Rousseff's inner circle figured that the best solution was to put Brazil's economy on the path to quick recovery. If that and other fail-safe measures failed, surely she could find another way to defend herself and stay in office until her term ended in 2018. And then, the thinking of Workers' Party supporters went, the likable and progressive Lula would get back the presidential sash, thus blocking politicians who were becoming increasingly popular with hard-right positions, such as congressman Jair Bolsonaro.

So, Rousseff put the bad news of impeachment in perspective. Being pressured by politicians, she always said, was much easier than enduring the torture she suffered during the military dictatorship of the 1970s, when she spent three years in jail. Just shy of her 68th birthday when the legislation was submitted, she had traveled a long, winding path to reach this point.

Born in 1947 in Belo Horizonte, the capital city of the central-eastern state of Minas Gerais, which borders Rio de Janeiro state, Rousseff grew up in an upper middle-class home. Her father, Petár Rusev, who would later change his name to Pedro Rousseff, was a Bulgarian immigrant who had arrived in Brazil in 1945. When he was 46, Pedro married Dilma Jane Coimbra da Silva, a teacher 26 years his junior. "Dilminha," or young Dilma, was the second of the couple's three children.

Early on, Rousseff showed an interest in reading and ballet, and would attend operas with her disciplined, austere and proud father — who friends and allies say was the most important figure in her life. She wore glasses from the time she was 12, but they didn't keep her from being a physically active kid. She and neighborhood friends would play on the tops of stone walls that separated houses. And her love of cycling started early: When she was 7 years old, her father bought her a yellow bicycle with an image of Mickey Mouse attached to the handlebars.

While Rousseff grew up comfortably, she was also keenly aware of the poverty around her. The year she was born, Belo Horizonte celebrated 50 years since its founding. Driven by mining and agriculture, the economy of the fledgling city flourished and the population increased rapidly, to more than 300,000. As is often the case in Brazil, however, development was uneven. Rapid industrialization brought poor people from rural areas faster than the infrastructure could be built to receive them.

People would sometimes knock on the door of Rousseff's family home to ask for work, money or food. One day, when a poor boy came to the door, a young Rousseff ripped a bill of cruzeiros (the currency at the time) in hopes of sharing it with the child. That drew a rebuke from her mother but an affectionate, light-hearted response from her father.[1]

When Rousseff was 15, her father, then 62, died of a heart attack. The businessman had left several properties, enough for the family to get by the next several years, but his sudden death had a huge impact on Rousseff.

Now a teenager, and no longer under her father's watchful eye, Rousseff began participating in socialist youth gatherings to talk about the country's turbulent political situation. There was a lot going on.

In 1960, Jânio da Silva Quadros, a populist former governor of São Paulo state, won the presidency on promises to sweep the country of corruption. His campaign symbol was a broom. But without a majority in Congress, combined with an eccentric personality that made governing difficult, Quadros resigned seven months into the job. Many historians believe that Quadros calculated that thousands of people would rise up and insist he return, giving him more leverage over Congress and the military. That never happened.

Coming from a family of landowners, João Goulart, who had been elected to the vice presidency in parallel with Quadros (at that time, Brazilians could vote for different tickets for president and vice president), took over after a compromise was reached in Congress. For many federal lawmakers, Goulart, from the Brazilian Labor Party, was too far to the left. It didn't help that Goulart was on a trade mission to communist China when Quadros resigned.

---

1. This and other details of Rousseff's early life come from Ricardo Batista Amaral's biography, *A Vida Quer É Coragem*, or *What Life Wants Is Courage*, published in 2011.

The Stage Is Set

After governing for two years alongside an appointed prime minister, per the agreement, in 1963 Goulart won a referendum that gave him full presidential powers. His administration moved further left, building ties with center-left political parties and simpatico foreign countries and initiating ambitious reforms around education, the tax code, voting rights and land redistribution, all the while clashing with leaders of more conservative currents in the country.

On April 1, 1964, when Rousseff was 16 years old, Goulart left the capital, Brasília, for Porto Alegre hours after rebel troops started moving to topple him. Brazil's Senate president declared the presidency vacant in a session that started at 2:40 a.m. the following day, as most of the country slept. There was almost no resistance, including from Goulart, who went into exile in Uruguay. A provisional president was sworn in only to be replaced soon after by Marshal Humberto Castelo Branco, the first dictator of the new regime.

That same year, Rousseff, a voracious reader, would leave her private school, the conservative Colégio Sion, for Central State High School, a public school where students often protested the dictatorship.

Like many of her generation in Brazil, Rousseff was heavily influenced by the 1959 Cuban Revolution. While the means to achieving the revolution's ideas were debated, what Fidel Castro was working toward resonated in a country with deep inequality.

By 1967, Rousseff joined the Revolutionary Marxist-Political Operation Organization, a spinoff of the Brazilian Socialist Party that brought several left-wing groups under its umbrella. The group was divided on how to engage with the dictatorship: Push for a constituent assembly to remake the constitution or take up armed struggle? Rousseff picked the latter.

By the late 1960s, as the dictatorship got more violent, Rousseff had joined the National Liberation Commands, moving weapons and overseeing some of the armed group's finances. During a meeting of the group, she met future husband Araújo in Rio de Janeiro (Her first marriage to journalist and fellow guerrilla fighter Cláudio Galeno de Magalhães Linhares, whom she wed at 19, had fallen apart).

Rousseff was arrested in January 1970 and tortured for several weeks by military officers who wanted her to name other group members. She withstood electric shocks, sleep deprivation and punches to her face. Then in August, Araújo was arrested.

Rousseff was sentenced to six years in prison. She had served three years when the Supreme Military Court reduced her sentence to just over two years. Araújo was still in jail in Porto Alegre, where Rousseff moved to be able to visit him. He was released in 1974 and the two decided to live together and later wed.

In the years ahead, Rousseff would return to university studies, have a daughter with Araújo and begin working with political parties and economic policy. Thirty years later, she was a Cabinet minister in Lula's administration, then moving to chief of staff and eventually president.

Now faced with her potential impeachment, even her most hardcore critics and adversaries knew that such a background meant that resigning was unlikely. All that she had endured as a prisoner simply made her too tough for that. If her detractors really wanted to get rid of her — and the number who did was quickly growing — she would have to be forced out.

And yet her allies liked to say that Rousseff was like a tube of toothpaste: When it seemed that nothing was left inside, pressure would bring much more out.

In her favor was the fact that she was not intoxicated by power like her predecessors. Many observers believed that her aspiration was simply to finish her presidency on Dec. 31, 2018, and go back to Porto Alegre to help raise her two grandsons.

"I was in jail for three years during the military rule. Does anyone with that experience spend a lot of time thinking of ifs?" Rousseff said during an interview with The Associated Press in 2017. "We just don't. I can only keep living."

Perhaps for all of these reasons, Rousseff was calm as she rode that Wednesday morning through Brasília, the capital founded as a planned city in 1960, a showcase of modernist architecture named City of Design by UNESCO. But Rousseff's calm didn't mean she would go down without a fight, no matter how politically isolated she had become. Even more so because her rise to the top in Latin America's most populous nation had been both unprecedented and unconventional.

"I have a historic responsibility here," she would repeat to her aides in the palace beginning on the first day of her presidency, Jan. 1, 2011. That day, arriving at the palace with her daughter Paula, Rousseff would help escort out Lula, who was leaving office with nearly a 90 percent approval rating.

In a country where politicians focus more on personality than ideology, and a machista culture pushes women to obsess about physical beauty, Rousseff was different. As a Cabinet member for many years, she wore big glasses, was sometimes overweight and never appeared worried about hairstyles and fashion like other women in government.

It was only during her first presidential campaign that she began sporting a more modern, shorter hairstyle. By the time she won her second term, she had lost the glasses and began losing weight. Following a radical diet prescribed by an Argentinian doctor, she lost 28 pounds (13 kilograms) that would never return.[2] Instead of eating cookies and taking extra work to bed as in the first years in office, the president was settling for palm heart soups, green salads and Netflix series to end her long, tense days.

There were other changes, too. Her personality was the opposite of chummy. Aides would describe a tough boss who didn't suffer fools and was quick to verbally lash out. By her second term, however, she was less

---

2. One of many articles on Rousseff's diet appeared in daily paper *Estadão* on March 2, 2015.

antagonistic when speaking with congressmen and reporters, probably at least in part because she knew her job was on the line.

She was cycling almost every day, an exercise routine established after a bout with cancer in 2010. She was also making more frequent comments on literature during surprisingly regular interviews. To supporters, it showed that Rousseff could still enjoy herself despite the dark clouds hovering over Brasília since her reelection and Brazil's seemingly never-ending political and economic crises. To adversaries, though, she came off as aloof and disengaged. In their view, how could the president, whose personality often came across as stoic, be cycling daily and making high-minded comments about books when many Brazilians were suffering?

Ironically, when Rousseff's approval ratings plunged to single digits in 2015, she often appeared more composed than when her popularity was at 80 percent during the early part of her first term. The calmer version of "Dilminha" was not the one that had gotten the attention of Lula in the 2002 presidential campaign when the former union leader finally was elected after three failed attempts. By then, Rousseff was already a respected economist and energy expert, but it was her work ethic on the campaign trail and frankness, which was also often a flaw, that landed her a Cabinet position as energy minister.

Her willingness to challenge other ministers, including some much closer to the president, and her clean record, a rarity in corruption-mired Brazilian politics, prompted Lula to elevate her to chief of staff in the wake of a massive corruption and influence-peddling scandal involving leadership of their Workers' Party in 2005. Rousseff's quick success as the main coordinator of the administration convinced the president that she should succeed him despite never having been elected to public office. Some Lula allies, such as former minister Ciro Gomes, argued that putting someone so inexperienced in the presidency was risky.

Still, she won handily in 2010. And her first years as president, when the region's largest and most powerful economy was still growing, went well enough. As the economy began to falter during the second half of her first mandate, however, there were worrisome signs, such as the massive street protests in June 2013.

What began in São Paulo over public transportation fare hikes morphed into anger over spending priorities, including the flashy ones Brazil made to be able to host the 2014 World Cup and 2016 Summer Olympics. Allegations of corruption were emerging from projects related to both events.

When the demonstrations started rocking Brazilian streets, it was clear that the nation, and its booming economy, which had raised millions from poverty, were both shifting. The protests began with leftists demanding better public services and they ended with conservatives, authoritarians and hard-right supporters pushing forward their agenda in a way that hadn't happened since the Workers' Party started winning presidential elections in 2002.

For many millennials who flooded the arteries of major cities for months, being rebellious meant advocating for a smaller state and challenging progressive politicians, many of whom had grown used to the perks of power. It also meant they could aim at a particular villain in Brasília, the once rogue and later establishment President Dilma Rousseff.

Despite some hits to her administration's popularity, Rousseff remained popular enough in 2014 to squeak out a reelection victory.

So why was it that just a year later, on Dec. 2, 2015, Brazil's lower chamber of Congress was beginning to consider impeachment? The stated reason was that Rousseff broke fiscal laws in managing the federal budget. But "pedaladas fiscais," loosely translated as "fiscal maneuvering" of the budget, always sounded like mumbo jumbo to most Brazilians.

If impeachment was a punishment looking for a crime, what would the crime be?

Was it that the economy, a world darling in the decade before she took power, had fallen into recession on her watch?

Was it a fallout from a massive corruption scandal at state oil company Petrobras, which would take on the notorious moniker "Car Wash?"

Had her vice president, as Rousseff would later suggest, really orchestrated a conspiracy to get her out of the way so he could take over?

Was the fault a stiff personality, which made it impossible for her to thrive in the old-boy backslapping environment common in Brasília?

Did her gender play a role? Many supporters argued that a man would never have been put through the same ordeal. President Fernando Collor de Mello had been impeached and resigned in 1992, but the corruption allegations against him were for personal gain.

Was it the cresting of a wave of anti-leftist sentiment and the growing strength of the right?

Or did a combination of these factors converge on Dec. 2, 2015, creating a nightmare scenario that shattered Dilma Rousseff's dream of support?

CHAPTER 2

The Speaker's Gambit

The decision by Dilma Rousseff's nemesis, Chamber of Deputies Speaker Eduardo Cunha, to open impeachment proceedings against her was anything but a straightforward attempt to snuff out presidential malfeasance. Instead, it was the culmination of many factors that would be laid bare in the months ahead.

"I am not happy at all doing this," Cunha said in his usually calm voice, speaking from the Salão Verde, which sits between the speaker's office and the chamber. The statement could not have been further from the truth. Cunha, his gray hair slicked back and donning rectangular-framed glasses, said that he had sought out several legal opinions, which concluded the president had committed crimes punishable with impeachment.

The evangelical preacher, keen on tweeting biblical verses, brought much of his own baggage to the table. For years, he had been dogged by allegations of corruption, including having illicit Swiss bank accounts holding millions of dollars. Cunha's explanation: The money was from his days selling canned beef in Africa.

He remained under the judicial microscope in 2015 — so much so that it was an open question whether he would stay out of jail long enough to actually submit the impeachment legislation.

Still, the man who was arguably Brazil's most powerful politician was anything but subtle. He and other adversaries, and even some luke-warm-allies-turned-enemies of Rousseff, had clearly been plotting how to bring about the president's political death.

"I felt outraged for her. She was being chased by criminals. She didn't deserve to go through all that," said Rousseff's ex-husband Araújo. Being treated for cancer and emphysema, he watched Cunha on television from the home where he and Rousseff had lived together in Porto Alegre. They had remained close friends and in fact planned to have lunch two days later. He knew it would be tense, that he would have to work hard to lighten the mood.

As he pondered the impeachment news, his mood shifted from out-rage. "I realized it would happen anyway. If not on that day, later," he said in an interview. "So, it would be for the best to get on with it and stop being blackmailed. It was somehow a relief."

Indeed, what happened that Wednesday was more than a year in the making.

Its roots went all the way back to the 2014 campaign, when polls showed two-thirds of Brazilians wanted a change after 12 years of Workers' Party governments. Facing this growing hunger for change, Rousseff gave her-self a political makeover of sorts.

She became more combative and used more leftist rhetoric. It was a bold move by her campaign: Promise that in a second term she would enact transformations she had not as an incumbent, such as pledges to break up media conglomerates. Supporters liked the new "Coração Valente," or "Braveheart," campaign motto, selling the incumbent president more like the rogue she was in the 1960s than the pragmatic and charisma-challenged leader she had become in office. For more moderate voters, Rousseff would often point out how she fought and overcame lymphatic cancer.

But bridges with business leaders and congressional allies were starting to crumble. Centrist backers did not join her in the demonization of adversaries, who of course demonized the president right back. Meanwhile, far-right currents gained traction on social media, setting the stage for what many argued would be Brazil's most divisive election since the return to democracy in the 1980s.

Through it all, Rousseff appeared so confident that she was on the right path that several press reports detailed how she was ignoring advice from Lula on the need for moderation. In fact, her predecessor was only a fixture in campaign commercials and events in the weeks before the first- and second-round votes.

A second term would bring about "more rights, reinforce women's autonomy, and a Brazil without (racial and gender) discrimination," Rousseff said during a campaign event in Belo Horizonte on Oct. 4, 2014.

Her main competitor, Sen. Aécio Neves, argued that a second Rousseff term would be a disaster. In particular, he focused on the economy and the mushrooming investigation into kickbacks. His overarching message: Standing with the current administration wasn't an option.

"Those who criticize, who are indignant about what is happening with Petrobras, with Electrobras (state oil and electric companies), are 'pessimists,'" Neves sarcastically said on campaign videos on his election website, referring to Rousseff's term for detractors. "Those who flatter the government are patriots."

Despite Rousseff's projection of confidence on the campaign trail, the economy was dipping. Commodity prices fell, and the president appeared incapable of responding in a way that reached increasing numbers of people who were hurting. Instead, she accused opposing lawmakers of planning unpopular austerity measures that ultimately she would also be ready to pursue in her second term.

And significantly, as she had all along, she relegated Vice President Michel Temer to a small role in the campaign. This, even though his backroom wheeling-and-dealing Brazilian Democratic Movement Party looked poised to once more win both the speakership in the Chamber of Deputies and presidency of the Senate.

To make matters worse for Rousseff and her own Workers Party, just a few miles (kilometers) away from the presidential palace, Brazilian politics had started to collapse at, of all places, Posto da Torre, a Brasília gas station not unlike countless others in the capital.

It began as an investigation into an illegal money transfer business being run at the station by owner Carlos Habib Chater and an associate, Alberto Youssef, a black-market money dealer who years before had been convicted for illegal money transfers abroad in a major bank scandal.

The first arrests were made during a March 2014 raid of the gas station. Over the next several months, many politicians and tycoons were arrested as the scope of the corruption came into view. It went way beyond some small-time hustling: it was a far-reaching and sophisticated graft scheme that extended all the way to Petrobras, one of Brazil's largest and most admired firms, and involved billions of dollars in bribes and illegal campaign financing. Although several parties were implicated, it was the Workers' Party that had the highest profile figures involved in what came to be known simply as the Car Wash investigation. After more than a decade in power, the party was increasingly looking spent.

Driving the investigation was a task force and judge in Curitiba, the capital of the southern state of Paraná, known for its efficient government services, mild weather and for being home to the world-famous Iguazu Falls (which are also partly in neighboring Argentina). The city of 2 million residents is a world away from São Paulo, the country's economic engine and biggest metropolis, or Rio de Janeiro, Brazil's signature city. By the end of 2014, however, Curitiba was becoming a center of Brazil's world thanks to the investigation, which posed a huge threat to Rousseff and her Workers' Party.

Yousseff, along with Paulo Roberto Costa, a top executive at Petrobras, would cut plea bargains with prosecutors that provided a window into the scope of the corruption. Authorities had begun focusing on Costa after discovering he had received a gift, a luxury Land Rover, from Yousseff, who had previously been convicted of money-laundering.

What Costa and Yousseff described in plea bargains was staggering: Top executives at multinational construction companies Odebrecht, OAS, Andrade Gutierrez and several others essentially formed a cartel that decided who would get multibillion-dollar building contracts doled out at various levels of government. Those contracts were greatly inflated. They had to be: The scheme involved millions of dollars in kickbacks for these businessmen and politicians and the coffers of many campaigns. Over more than a decade, prosecutors estimated that several billion dollars were paid out in bribes. Odebrecht was so deeply entrenched in the scheme that it even had a department dedicated to bribes.

Rousseff was never directly implicated or named in the alleged bribe-taking. While she also maintained she didn't know what was going on, it was a defense that many Brazilians had a hard time accepting. In the decade before taking office in 2011, she had held several top positions in government. She was Minister of Energy, which oversees Petrobras, between 2003 and 2005, a time when prosecutors say the graft scheme was alreadyinplace.Ifsayingshedidn'tknowdefiedbeliefformanyBrazilians, the possibility that she really didn't know was perhaps even worse.

In the face of so much stealing, could she really not have noticed? Was she really that inept? Or had she been quietly trying to remove rotten apples and not publicly speak about what had been going on when her mentor was in office? These were questions that many Brazilians were asking themselves.

Two days before the 2014 elections, the magazine *Veja* published an issue with a provocative headline. "They Knew Everything." Under the headline were pictures of Rousseff and Lula.[3]

Rousseff went on national television hours before polls were open to say the report was false. And the story in *Veja*, once a hard-hitting and serious news magazine that many argue had become more tabloid than reputable journalism, was thin at best.

Despite the hits her reputation took, when Election Day came Rousseff still managed to win a narrow victory. But the celebrations didn't last long.

Right after she beat Neves 51.64 percent to 48.36 percent, members of the opposition started talking about a recount. They called for scrutinizing electronic ballots. Then they threatened to take the winning ticket to court for alleged illegal campaign financing.

Some on the growing hard-right even advocated for military intervention.

An echo of that last notion appeared in a book that Rousseff was reading at the time, according to her ex-husband and media reports, and which she mentioned during interviews herself. It was a biography of former President Getúlio Vargas, a populist leader who committed suicide in 1954 amid a political crisis that sought to remove him from office. Rousseff said she was struck by a quote related to Vargas' second run for president in the 1950s. The quote, from right-wing Rio de Janeiro Gov.

---

3. *Veja* magazine published this piece on Oct. 23, 2014.

Carlos Lacerda, a friend of the military, summed up how she felt she was being treated by opponents in Congress.

"Mr. Getúlio Vargas should not be a candidate for president," said Lacerda. "If he is a candidate, he should not be elected. If he is elected, he should not be inaugurated. If he is inaugurated, we should make a revolution to stop him from governing."

By late 2014, the opposition's attempts to keep Rousseff from beginning a second term were not bearing fruit. However, when Cunha beat Rousseff's candidate to become speaker in early 2015, the attempt to bring forward an impeachment case looked viable: As speaker, Cunha had the sole right to put impeachment legislation before the Chamber of Deputies. But what could be a credible challenge? That was the main question.

There were many detractors ready to come up with an answer. By mid-2015, dozens of impeachment petitions were being crafted. Bolsonaro, the hard-right deputy and frequent Rousseff critic, was the first legislator to submit impeachment legislation: His was based on alleged involvement of Workers' Party officials in the growing Car Wash scandal.

Bolsonaro argued that Rousseff had committed the crime of "neglect" for not adopting "repressive measures to fight the cancer of corruption within her administration." Bolsonaro cited the sale of an oil refinery in Pasadena, Texas, as an alleged shady deal overseen by the leftist president and also argued that a program to bring foreign doctors to impoverished Brazilian communities gave "hefty amounts to the Cuban government."

Cunha said he wouldn't consider Bolsonaro's petition because Rousseff's second term had only just begun. For Rousseff to be impeached, it had to be for something she did in her current term, which began Jan. 1, 2015.[4] That didn't give him a long period from which to draw.

Rousseff and Cunha had a mutually hateful relationship going back

---

4. Cunha recounts some of the petitions, including Bolsonaro's, in his book, *Bye, Dear: A Diary of Impeachment*, published in 2021.

15 years. She had done all she could to stop Cunha from rising up to the third most important office in the land. And Cunha, despite being a friend of Vice President Temer and a supporter of the popular Lula administrations, made no effort to support the Rousseff-Temer ticket during the reelection campaign.

Political observers expected Rousseff to tread carefully with Cunha, as he was unpredictable and emboldened to act. Even though it would be very difficult for Cunha to remove her, and in the end it could hurt him, it was also unlikely that Rousseff could outmaneuver the most resourceful lawmaker in Brazil.

There would be numerous hurdles getting impeachment legislation through Congress. Two-thirds of the 513 members of the Chamber of Deputies would have to vote for the opening of the impeachment process. If the petition prevailed in the lower chamber, it would then move to the Senate. For Rousseff to ultimately be removed, two thirds of the Senate would have to vote in favor during a trial overseen by the chief justice of the Supreme Federal Tribunal. At any stage, the top court could intervene to keep her in charge.

Beyond the procedural hurdles, however, there was a much larger and more basic challenge for opponents: No clear proof of wrongdoing by Dilma Rousseff.

The original 65-page impeachment petition, which would become the basis of the measure considered by Congress, began by arguing that Brazil was in crisis and Rousseff was guilty of both "criminal" and "moral" crimes. Over several pages, it recounted high-profile arrests made in the Car Wash investigation, arguing that Rousseff's different roles in government over the years meant she had to know what was happening.

What's more, Rousseff had close relationships with people who were implicated, according to the petition. For example, the Petrobras executive whose plea bargain implicated many elites in Car Wash, Paulo

Roberto Costa, had attended the wedding of Rousseff's daughter, according to the petition.

With broad yet vague accusations as a canvas, the legislation specifically accused Rousseff of two actions that were "crimes of responsibility," defined in the constitution generally as several different actions a president might do to deliberately undermine the state.

First, Rousseff was accused of issuing six unnumbered decrees of supplemental credit in 2015 to be allocated to social programs that allegedly would help shore up her support at the beginning of her second term. These totaled $18.5 billion Brazilian reals (US $6.9 billion at the time) and didn't have authorization from Congress, breaking the Law of Fiscal Responsibility. To authorize these credits and comply with budgeting laws, Rousseff ordered the reduction of revenue targets, according to the legislation.

The government had sent a bill to Congress in July 2015 to change the annual estimate of the deficit for the fiscal year, but it was not approved until December. Proponents of impeachment said the attempt to adjust the targets showed Rousseff knew what she had done and was trying to clean it up. Rousseff officials said that the decrees and subsequent legislation, all happening in the middle of a recession with plummeting revenues, were an attempt to provide flexibility to the government sectors receiving and using the money.

What's more, authorizing credit didn't mean actual spending. In sum, Rousseff's administration argued this was budgeting adaptations and minutiae, not sleight-of-hand maneuvering for political gain.

Second, the administration was accused of orchestrating illegal credit operations, a practice called "pedaladas fiscais," or fiscal maneuvering, between 2011 and 2014. It worked like this: Instead of loans being originated by the National Treasury and then processed and distributed by state banks, the loans started with the state banks. Doing that allowed the government to fill budget gaps without reflecting that debt on its balance sheet, according to the petition.

Rousseff opponents said this was done to fund social programs and bolster the president's 2014 reelection chances. However, not only had previous presidential administrations and state administrations done similar maneuvering, for such an action to be considered a "crime of responsibility," there had to be proof that the president willfully participated and had ill intent.

The alleged fiscal maneuvering included transactions involving Plano Safra, a government program that provided subsidies to small farmers and was run by the Ministry of Finance. There was no evidence that Rousseff had directed any of the actions; orders for the subsidies didn't require her signature.

In any case, while the "pedaladas fiscais" would be frequently mentioned by detractors, they were largely excised from the final impeachment legislation being considered since Cunha had limited its scope to only alleged wrongdoing in Rousseff's second term that began in 2015.

Merits of the case aside, in private discussions at the Brasília home of conservative deputy Heráclito Fortes, lawmakers and legal scholars started discussing ways to get the president out. "Impeachment is a political process" became their motto. If removing Rousseff didn't work, at the very least they would reduce the chances of a Lula comeback in the 2018 elections.

Cunha, whose two-year term as speaker would give him plenty of time to take aim at Rousseff, attended many of these meetings.[5] He also held secret gatherings of his own with key allies, politicians whose campaigns he had supported.

He made clear that he would do everything in his power to make

---

5. Daily paper *Estadão* reported on the meetings and attendees in an article published April 16, 2016.

governing impossible for the administration and make Rousseff appear ineffective. He put to vote proposals that were fiscally inviable, so-called "bomb-bills." For example, one measure passed in September 2015, at a time Brazil desperately needed to trim its budget and bring some confidence to investors, approved an extra expenditure of 22 billion Brazilian reals (US $7 billion) per year, nearly the same size of a budget cut being suggested by Rousseff.

Cunha was a member of and gave a boost to a large group of lawmakers who wanted right-leaning legislation, the so-called B.B.B. (bullets, beef and Bibles) caucus. Under Cunha's direction, the Chamber of Deputies considered bills to include language in the constitution that a family is formed by "a man and a woman" and increase the hurdles for pregnant women who had been raped to get abortions (in most instances, abortion was and continues to be illegal in Brazil). Much of the B.B.B.-agenda was blocked in the chamber by members of Rousseff's Workers' Party or coalitions in the Senate. And some of these initiatives were long-shots or simply aimed at firing up the base, as they went against already established law, like gay marriage, allowed in Brazil since 2011.

Cunha also blocked probes against himself and allies in Congress while calling for investigations against the government and its allies. Throughout much of 2015, he successfully pulled off something that only the most skilled politician could even attempt: encourage protesters to take to the streets to show their anger at corruption while he himself was increasingly under a microscope for corruption.

Some protesters at anti-Rousseff demonstrations also called for Cunha's ouster, and leaders of online organizing groups went so far as to acknowledge that while Cunha's time to face justice might come, first they would focus their energies on Rousseff.[6] After all, Cunha's plan dovetailed nicely with the hopes of anti-left groups: Kick the president out by August 2015.

But then came a development that would influence both his fate and that of Rousseff: A vote in the ethics committee on whether Cunha could continue in office in light of the corruption investigations against him.

Understanding that alleged corruption requires a brief look backward. Similar to that of Rousseff, Cunha's political rise paralleled major changes taking place in Brazil. By the late 1970s, the dictatorship began softening, and pro-democracy movements were growing. A new generation, different from Rousseff's guerrilla friends, could aspire to democracy without guns. Another big change was that being close to the military no longer meant success in business.

Young economist Eduardo Cosentino da Cunha was a quick study of these changes sweeping over the country. While he worked at the Rio offices of accounting firm Arthur Andersen, he also did taxes for politicians. That gave him deep knowledge about Brazil's complex tax code and how to operate offshore accounts, skills that were key for his political career but would eventually bring him trouble.

Lobbyist Jorge Luz, a business partner, played a large role in getting Cunha into politics. Luz had the respect of then Brazilian President José Sarney. A specialist in energy and deeply involved with Petrobras, the multilingual Luz was also keen on offshore accounts and international operations. He thought Eduardo, or "Eddie," was a fundraising genius.

Through Luz, in 1989 Cunha became one of the main fundraisers for presidential candidate Fernando Collor de Mello. Shortly afterward,

---

6. In this BBC Brasil article published on Aug. 14, 2015, leaders of online groups talk about their strategy to focus on Rousseff despite mounting allegations against Cunha.

Cunha became the head of Rio's state-run phone company. Accusations that he mishandled bank accounts of the company ended in his resignation in 1991. That was the first of a series of corruption allegations that followed him to Brazil's Congress and, in 2015, to the speakership of the Chamber of Deputies.

And just as his campaign against Rousseff was nearing a climax, bad news for Cunha came from Switzerland: A bank found US $5 million in an account linked to him. That directly contradicted a statement to fellow lawmakers not long before.

"I don't have any kind of bank account anywhere else but the one I declared in my taxes," he had told colleagues in November 2015.

Members of Congress largely stay out of each other's personal business — congressional investigations about members of either chamber are rare. But lying publicly to colleagues is looked down upon.

After much delay, key members of the Chamber of Deputies ethics committee made public on that fateful Wednesday in December their belief that Cunha should be investigated and, if found guilty, stripped of his seat. That vote wouldn't happen until later in the month, but indicating their stance made clear which way things would go.

Until that day, the 20-member ethics commission had been split. Three votes — all members of Rousseff's Workers' Party — would be decisive. Pressure had been on to spare Cunha, at least until the threat of impeachment had passed. Regardless, few believed that the unpredictable speaker would spare Rousseff. If he didn't open proceedings at that moment, he would surely do it later. That looming commission decision had been a cold war between Cunha and the administration.

"When Cunha is elected speaker (in February 2015), he starts a process of constant threats," José Eduardo Cardozo, at the time justice minister, recalled during an interview. "He was worried about Car Wash getting to him. He demanded that the government stop the investigations, and wanted me to fire the head of the federal police. Then he said he wanted to get rid of me because I was allegedly conspiring with Attorney General Rodrigo Janot to take him down."

The news of the ethics committee members' decision quickly spread nationwide. Within a few hours, Cunha called Rousseff's chief of staff, Jaques Wagner, to inform him that the president's job would soon be on the line.

Wagner told Rousseff that Cunha would give a press conference after 6 p.m. to talk about the impeachment case.

"At least we can get this over with," Rousseff said, according to Olimpio Neto, one of her press aides. And the embattled president immediately started preparing her counterattack.

She called a meeting of Cabinet members to energize every minister and every element of her multiparty governing coalition. Eleven ministers from six different parties were present, and she asked all to speak. Rousseff said she wanted her Cabinet next to her at the presidential palace to respond to Cunha and say that she was ready for the fight.[7]

The set was prepared. A banner that was supposed to hang behind her was shifted from its original position so only the word Brazil, in green, would be seen above the president. When she spoke directly into the camera, she didn't mention her nemesis by name but there could be no doubt who she was talking about.

"I have committed no illegal act. There is no suspicion that I diverted public money," Rousseff said matter-of-factly, clearly trying to minimize the accusations against her. "I do not have offshore bank accounts. I did not hide private possessions from the public. I never coerced nor tried to coerce institutions or people to satisfy my interests."

---

7. Published by *G1* news portal Dec. 15, 2015.

The Speaker's Gambit

At the end of her speech, all the ministers walked behind her silently. No one needed to say what they all noticed before the dramatic scene even unfolded: that one key member of government was notably absent.

This was Michel Temer, Rousseff's vice president and next in line if the president were removed.

CHAPTER 3

'A Decorative Vice President'

"Madam President,
'Verba volant, scripta manent.'
Words fly, writings remain."

When Vice President Michel Miguel Elias Temer Lulia decided to write a letter to show his dissatisfaction to boss Dilma Rousseff, all of his distinctive traits were on display: a proud knowledge of Latin, his command of an almost arcane Portuguese diction, pompous academic origins and expertise in the minutiae of Congress.

'A Decorative Vice President'

It had been less than a week since Eduardo Cunha opened the impeachment proceedings when Temer's allegedly private letter started flying around Brasília.

"That is why I write to you. Very much due to the intense news of the last few days and everything that gets to my ears about the conversations at the palace," Temer began the letter, dated Dec 7, 2015, after his Latin intro. *"This is a personal letter. I am venting in a way that I should have done long ago."*

It had been several months since Temer started distancing himself from the president, just like a big part of his centrist Brazilian Democratic Movement Party (PMDB). Behind the scenes, he reportedly used meetings with politicians to complain about the lack of trust that Rousseff and her inner circle had in him and in the junior coalition partner. In public, the vice president started making comments that suggested he was applying for the top job.

"Someone needs to bring everyone together," Temer told reporters during a press conference in August without mentioning his boss as a person up for the task. Though increasingly suspicious, Rousseff later replied that together they could do that job.

The malaise peaked when Rousseff gathered her ministers to try to show unity in the face of Cunha's attack, and Temer didn't even show up. The president initially shrugged it off, telling CBN radio the day the legislation was submitted that she didn't distrust her silent VP "even by a millimeter."

Then the letter came out.

"First off, I tell you that it is not necessary for me to make public boasts of my loyalty (to you). I have shown it over these five years.

"It is an institutional loyalty regarding Article 79 of the federal constitution. I know the role of the vice president. To my natural

discretion, I added that derived from that constitutional device.

"However, I was always aware of the absolute distrust that you and your entourage have toward me and PMDB. Distrust that is incompatible with what we have done to keep personal and party support to your administration."

The first paragraphs of the letter were enough to show that Temer was no longer with her. He clearly couldn't resist expressing his frustration — and showing his pedantic side — and much of what would come next in the letter was not for the supposed recipient (Rousseff said it was never "sent (to her) but leaked").

Article 79, which is just a few sentences, explains the duties of the vice president, something Rousseff clearly didn't need spelled out. One clause says the vice president "will help the president with special assignments whenever he is called upon." Temer seemed to be focused on the principal part of the article: In the case of an impediment, the vice president will substitute and replace the president.

When he decided not to stand with Rousseff at that key moment, was it because he was truly resentful, like many other lawmakers in Brasília frustrated with her? Or did he see an opportunity?

Largely unknown on the national stage before becoming vice president, Temer had risen from humble origins and had a career trajectory that spanned several decades. Born in 1940 in Tietê, a small city about 90 miles (145 kilometers) northwest of São Paulo, Temer was the youngest of eight children whose parents had immigrated from Lebanon. After high school, he followed his older brothers in studying law, graduating from the University of São Paulo's law school in 1963.

Unlike Rousseff, Temer stayed neutral about the 1964 coup, largely avoiding politics and instead deepening his knowledge of the law. He completed a doctorate in public law, taught classes and wrote a handful of books on the subject.

'A Decorative Vice President'

By the 1980s, Temer was moving into politics. After working as a state prosecutor, in 1983 he was named São Paulo's attorney general. He would later serve as the state's secretary of public security for Gov. Franco Montoro, a leader of Brazil's redemocratization process.

In 1987, Temer would serve the first of six terms in the Chamber of Deputies, three times being elected speaker. His deep background in law made him a natural to be part of the National Constituent Assembly that drafted and approved the 1988 constitution. He would also become president of the PMDB, a party that included liberals and leftists during the military dictatorship but had evolved into a gelatinous mix of conservatives and centrists over the years.

His laid-back mannerisms earned him the nickname "butler," and he said that he hadn't used swear words since an early age, a recommendation of his parents. For all his mild manner, he clearly had great influence among his peers. A 2009 survey of members of the lower chamber and Senate named him the most influential member of Congress.[8]

Still, if most Brazilians knew Temer for anything when he was Rousseff's running mate in 2010, it was probably for his marriage to a former beauty pageant contestant nearly 43 years his junior. Temer met Marcela Tedeschi Araújo in 2002 at a PMDB convention in São Paulo. A year later, when she was 20 and he was about to turn 63, they wed.

"It is enough to stress that in the last (PMDB) convention only 59.9% voted for this alliance. And they only did so, I dare to say, because I was the candidate for reelection as vice president."

Historically, the PMDB has not revolved around ideology at all. Many political analysts have long argued that party leaders and congressional

---

8. An article in *Folha de S. Paulo* in October 2009 reported on the results of the vote among lawmakers as to who was the most influential.

seat holders are basically a group of local bosses who work together to get perks from the central government — and keep members elected.

During Brazil's 1964-1985 military dictatorship, there were only two legal parties: MDB (which would later add "P" for "Party" to its name) and the ruling Arena, or Alliance for National Renovation. While the latter governed the country, MDB was allowed to exist with a mixture of moderates, liberals, communists, leftists and so on.

After the return of democracy in 1985, the party, now PMDB, had representation in every presidential cabinet, but rarely had a presidential candidate. It would be a stretch to call Temer the main leader of a party that had none. However, since the 1990s, he had been a galvanizing figure astute at helping fellow members get government positions along with earmarks for their constituents. Perhaps most importantly for him, he did this while always maintaining good relations with most in the party.

"I have kept the unity of PMDB supporting your administration by using the political prestige that I have due to the credibility and respect that I have earned in the party. All of this did not generate confidence in me. It generated distrust and contempt from the administration."

Temer was made candidate for vice president in 2010 because Rousseff and her mentor Lula wanted three things: a more centrist look for the former guerrilla fighter at the top of the ticket, more free airtime for political ads on television (Brazilian parties and candidates get airtime based on the number of seats their party holds in Congress) and the support of a large chunk of PMDB in Congress. When Lula was elected in 2002, PMDB had been on an opposing center-right ticket led by José Serra.

Under Brazil's political system, it's rare that a presidential candidate can be competitive with a running mate from the same party. On the campaign trail, an alliance between differing parties improves the chances of winning an election, as Brazil's population is very diverse and the country is larger than the continental United States. A deal with PMDB gave Rousseff an alliance with the party with the most federal lawmakers and mayors, key to getting out the vote in major cities and Brazil's many rural areas.

Still, there were questions about whether the alliance made sense beyond the numbers. Rousseff's program was basically sticking to what Lula had done while hoping for the best. PMDB was not in it to defend any specific policy.

The arrangement worked well enough during Rousseff's first term, but her troubled reelection in 2014 brought new risks. After arguably Brazil's most divisive presidential elections up to that point, and the election of the most conservative Congress in decades, PMDB's support became even more important. But, as Temer pointed out in his letter to Rousseff, he and his party were largely ignored, contradicted or publicly overturned by the president and her aides. Temer also did the same to her a few times, but at that crucial point what mattered most was his narrative, not hers.

> *"I spent the first four years of the administration as a decorative VP. You, Madam, know that. I lost the political leading role that I once had and that could have been used by the administration. I was only called to decide the votes of PMDB and the political crisis."*

Since 1994, two political parties have dominated Brazilian politics, at least in terms of the presidency. Founded in 1980, Lula's Workers' Party put the former metal worker as its main leader from the very beginning. Rousseff was elected on the back of Lula's huge popularity and a still booming Brazilian economy.

On the other side was former President Fernando Henrique Cardoso and his Brazilian Social Democratic Party, known by its acronym PSDB. Members of PSDB, called "tucanos" because the party symbol is a toucan, created the party in 1988 when social democrats and liberals broke away from an already scandal-prone PMDB. Temer never left his party, but maintained close relations with many who did. In that way, he was one of the many bridges between the two.

Whenever someone in PMDB began garnering attention and considering a presidential run, Temer was one of the first to reject that move within the party. The vice president, like other key members of his party, instead acted as kingmakers to center-right and center-left administrations.

After all, the only two PMDB presidential candidates failed miserably in their attempts to win office. Pro-democracy leader Ulysses Guimarães, who many expected to be Brazil's first president after the end of the dictatorship, finished the 1989 elections in 7th place with less than 5 percent of the vote. It was almost the same result five years later when conservative São Paulo governor Orestes Quercia was the PMDB's candidate for the presidency.

"Never was I nor PMDB called to discuss the economy or political formulations for the country; we were mere accessories, secondary, subsidiary."

Personal slights were among Temer's laundry list of complaints, making clear that he and Rousseff never got along. Instead, they were the product of an arranged marriage. Like so many marriages, arranged or otherwise, this one was coming to an end. Temer wanted a divorce but he clearly didn't plan on being the one to leave the house.

"You Madam, in your second term, at the last minute, did not keep the Ministry of Civil Aviation, where Wellington Moreira Franco did a great job that was praised in the World Cup. You knew that was an appointment that I made. You wanted to belittle me. I registered this fact the following day on the phone."

'A Decorative Vice President'

In late 2014, in a reshuffle ahead of beginning her second term, Rousseff replaced Franco, a former Rio de Janeiro governor and close friend of Temer's, with Eliseu Padilha, a former transportation minister who was also a Temer ally. Since both men were close to Temer, the vice president's beef was clearly that he had appointed one of them and Rousseff the other. And getting Padilha into the administration would turn out to help Temer in a big way.

In April 2015, Rousseff named Temer her minister for congressional relations. The role gave the vice president an entire map of who was doing what and key appointments throughout Congress. Temer left the job in August without accomplishing much. In his place, he left Padilha.

Padilha, who many lawmakers pointed to as a key impeachment-vote strategist, left the job one day after Cunha opened the impeachment proceedings. Brasília insiders understood that move as a likely breakup between the president and the vice president, but Temer's letter went even farther than most disgruntled PMDB members had been dreaming about. Temer's defense of Padilha, who according to the vice president was treated badly by the administration, was really a declaration of war.

> *"In the episode of Eliseu Padilha, more recently, he left the Cabinet due to several 'slights' ending with what the administration did to him, a minister, by removing with no prior notice an appointment with a technocratic profile that he, the minister of that area, had made to Brazil's civil aviation agency. That showed (everyone) that a) it was retaliation against me; b) he left because he is part of an alleged 'conspiracy.'"*

Advisors who warned Lula years before that no one from PMDB should ever be in the line of succession for the presidency said the same about giving the keys of the administration to the vice president by naming him minister of congressional relations. "He is going to give jobs to his friends, find out what each party has and wants and then wash his hands," former minister Ciro Gomes said.[9] "That is exactly what Temer did only four months after becoming minister."

In that same interview published the day before Temer's letter came out, Gomes went so far as to call Temer the "captain of the coup" when referring to the building impeachment push.

> *"When you, Madam, made an appeal for me to take over the political coordination in a moment that the administration had very little prestige, I did so and we got, I and Padilha, the fiscal tightening approved. It is a hard issue because it relates to both workers and businessmen. We did not hesitate. The country was at stake. When the tightening was approved, nothing that we did was followed by the administration. All the agreements made in Congress were not fulfilled. We organized more than 60 meetings of leaders and parties requesting support with our credibility. We were forced to abandon that coordination."*

There was rarely unity in PMDB, even under Temer, and leaders of the Workers' Party and PSDB knew how to take advantage of that. When Cunha lured the most conservative members of PMDB to the opposition, Rousseff worked to garner support among those who disliked the speaker, Temer and their inner circle. Pleasing and pushing away factions of PMDB had become a key part of Brazil's political game for decades. It usually wasn't personal; it was merely how business was done.

> *"I am the PMDB chairman and you Madam decided to ignore me by calling leader Leonardo Picciani and his father to make a deal without any communication with your vice president and the chairman of the party. Both ministers, you know, were nominated by them. And you*

---

9. Gomes' interview by Rede TV was published by news portal *O Povo Online* on Dec. 6, 2015.

'A Decorative Vice President'

Madam didn't have any problem removing from the Cabinet deputy Edinho Araújo, a deputy from São Paulo and linked to me."

In November 2015, Rousseff wanted to break PMDB from within. She approached the scandal-prone Picciani clan, which held key positions in Rio de Janeiro and in Congress. With support of the Piccianis, the president could show PMDB it would be difficult to topple her and would also present speaker Cunha with a natural rivalry in his home state. The symbol of the alliance was concrete: The Piccianis appointed two ministers to Rousseff's Cabinet. That move would also eventually fail.

"Since I am a democrat, I do, Madam President, talk to the opposition. I always did in the 24 years that I spent in Congress. Besides, the first executive order of the tightening was approved thanks to eight votes of the Democrats, six of the Brazilian Socialist Party and three of the Green Party, and I should remind you that the order was approved by only 22 votes. I am criticized for that, in a mistaken perception of our system. And it was for good reason that in two opportunities I stressed that we should reunite the country. The palace decided to spread (misinformation) and criticize."

At first, Brazil's opposition believed that the best way to remove Rousseff was to seek an electoral court ruling that would strip both her and Temer from their positions for alleged campaign finance violations in the 2014 election. But interest in pursuing the campaign finance route waned and all but disappeared over the course of 2015.

Opposition lawmakers were often seen at night visiting the vice presidential residence, Jaburu's Palace, with local media capturing the comings and goings during stakeouts. While little beyond generalities were made public about the meetings, more lawmakers began publicly endorsing impeachment proceedings against Rousseff, which would leave Temer in the top job.

Temer's entourage publicly said the meetings were to try to break up the gridlock in Congress, a legislative agenda coordinated by Cunha. And Temer would frequently deny that he was involved in planning Rousseff's impeachment. Still, it stands to reason that during those meetings Temer was gauging his chances of taking over and was perhaps even whipping votes.[10]

> *"I remember that, still, you Madam kept a meeting of two hours with Vice President Joe Biden, with whom I built a good friendship, in your inauguration without inviting me, which led your aides to a question: what happened in a meeting with the vice president of the United States in which Brazil's (vice president) was not present? Before, in the episode of the American 'espionage,' when the conversations restarted, you Madam told the justice minister to talk to the U.S. vice president. All of that points to an absolute lack of trust."*

Biden and Rousseff met in Brasília on Jan. 1, 2015, during the second-term inauguration of Rousseff and Temer. Temer was clearly miffed that he wasn't invited, and he was also upset about being left out of the repairing of relations between the U.S. and Brazil after leaked U.S. National Security Agency documents in 2013 showed that Rousseff's personal communication had been hacked. Rousseff had been enraged about the reports and canceled an upcoming trip to Washington. A chill settled over the U.S.-Brazil relationship for a few years.

One day after skipping Rousseff's attempt to show unity in the face

---

10. Magazine *Piauí's* February 2016 issue examines the lawmakers who visited Temer's residence in the months after the impeachment legislation was submitted.

of impeachment proceedings, Temer met with the president. Rousseff said publicly that Temer promised to help her defense. Chief of Staff Jaques Wagner gave a press conference to praise Temer's "long trajectory of being a democrat and a constitutional scholar" and said that the backdoor politician "does not see any basis for this impeachment case" against Rousseff.

On two occasions before the letter came out, Temer flatly denied having said that. Cunha would later say every step he took at the time was advised and agreed to by Temer, but the vice president denied that.[11]

"More recently, a conversation of ours (two of the top authorities of the country) was publicized and in an untruthful way without any connection with the content of the conversation."

A first sign that Temer wanted a role in policy-making came in October 2015, when the impeachment negotiations were already at full speed in Congress. With the help of the liberal section of his party, a pro-business document called "A Bridge to the Future," filled with suggestions of austerity measures, was released.

Rousseff didn't see it as advice from the junior partners on what to do to overcome the political and economic turmoil. She saw it as an open attempt to lure business leaders toward Temer, a man who made his career as a moderate but was now talking about austerity measures and reforms, which he had not done the previous five years.

"Even the program, 'A Bridge to the Future,' which was applauded by society with proposals that could be used to recover the economy and regain trust, was seen as a disloyal maneuver."

---

11. Cunha made the claims in a letter he wrote that was published by news magazine *Exame* on April 18, 2017.

Approaching the Picciani clan to break PMDB from inside was not Rousseff's first move to divide and conquer the junior partner. She was tired of repeating the vicious circle of encountering roadblocks to enacting her agenda, having to offer more cabinet positions to PMDB leaders, seeing scandals erupt and then getting in trouble again. That is what led her in 2012 to encourage PMDB members who rarely disagreed with the administration to join a new party, the Social Democratic Party, or PSD.

Led by former São Paulo mayor and Cabinet member Gilberto Kassab, the PSD was no different from PMDB. "We will not be on the left, on the right or in the center," Kassab said after its founding in 2011.[12]

The attempt to divide PMDB failed, and Rousseff had to stick with her vice president for the 2014 reelection campaign. Rousseff's move was still fresh in the memories of PMDB leaders when the president faced the ultimate challenge, the impeachment effort.

> *"PMDB is aware that the administration seeks to promote its split, which it has already tried in the past with no success. You Madam know that, as PMDB chairman, I must keep a cautious silence with the objective of seeking what I always seek: party unity."*

Writing the letter and leaking it was arguably the boldest move of Temer's political career up to that point. He was always known for his moderation, so his finger-pointing rhetoric and willingness to discuss and even air petty frustrations stunned some of his allies. With it, he signaled to Brazilians that he was running for president and that he saw himself as part of the solution to the country's ongoing political crisis.

When his fellow PMDB members heard Rousseff allies make offers, just like those they had heard president after president make, they started coming up with a simple answer: Why help a failing leader in

---

12. Quoted by daily *Estadão* on March 29, 2011.

exchange for government positions when the party could have all of them under Temer?

The bridge to the future apparently could only go in one direction. With growing public sentiment against Rousseff and her Workers' Party, whoever looked set to push them out would have the support of a vast part of Brazilian society, many media organizations and, of course, Congress. But that would only materialize when the ousting happened, Temer suggested.

"After these critical moments, I am sure that the country will have the tranquility to grow and consolidate social achievements.

"Finally, I know that you Madam have no trust in me and in PMDB today, and you won't have it tomorrow. I regret it, but that is my conviction.

Respectfully,

\ L TEMER

To Your Excellency, Madam

Doctor DILMA ROUSSEFF

President of the Republic of Brazil

Palácio do Planalto"

CHAPTER 4

Rules of Engagement

When Luiz Edson Fachin was nominated as a justice of the Supreme Federal Tribunal by Rousseff in May 2015, the outcry by Brazil's opposition was so loud that for the first time in decades there was real concern that an appointee wouldn't get the typical rubber stamp from the Senate. After all, the soft-spoken law professor of Universidade Federal do Paraná wasn't a mere scholar. He had been an open supporter of Rousseff, even appearing in an ad for her campaign in 2010.

"We support Dilma," Fachin said before hundreds of people during a rally.[13] "So we can continue together in the construction of a country that is capable of growing and bringing development for everyone. The administration that we want is the one that has been able to preserve democratic institutions and the one that never tolerated authoritarians."

Only months after Rousseff eked out a reelection victory, senators had to decide whether Fachin deserved one of the 11 seats on the country's highest court. Senators, even in the opposition, were typically loath to vigorously oppose a justice nominee who could stay on the job until age 75 — plenty of time to make their lives difficult later. And in the end, even many Rousseff opponents rolled over when it came time to decide on Fachin's confirmation. He was approved 52-27, giving Rousseff a rare victory in the first year of her second term.

Political analysts figured Fachin would be a Rousseff ally in the upcoming impeachment fight, but with just one vote he probably wouldn't be able to sway the process. In short, Cunha allies and impeachment backers shrugged at Fachin's appointment and breathed easy. Then something happened that rocked their confidence: When Rousseff challenged Cunha's impeachment roadmap in the Supreme Federal Tribunal, Fachin was picked in a lottery to oversee the case.

Brazil's constitution broadly lays out the impeachment process. If a president is accused of committing a "crime of responsibility," defined as an action to purposely undermine the state, the Chamber of Deputies votes on whether to ratify the admissibility of an impeachment petition. For it to be deemed admissible, a two-thirds majority must vote in favor.

If that happens, the legislation then goes to the Senate. For the president to ultimately be removed, two thirds of the senators must vote in favor after a trial overseen by the chief justice of the Supreme Federal Tribunal. However, the constitution doesn't specifically lay out what

---

13. The 2010 video was posted and written about in daily *Folha de S.Paulo* on April 14, 2015.

steps, if any, should happen between the vote in the lower chamber and final trial in the Senate.

In 1992, in the country's only previous impeachment proceeding since redemocratization in the 1980s, the Chamber of Deputies voted to impeach President Fernando Collor de Mello amid a series of corruption allegations against him personally. In the Senate, by an act of its chairman, Collor was put on trial directly. The president would resign before the Senate voted on removal. However, even after that, the Senate decided to formally vote to remove him.

Similar to what happened in 1992, Cunha's impeachment roadmap called for an immediate suspension of Rousseff from office in the event that the Chamber of Deputies voted in favor of the measure. In other words, the Senate's job would then be to try Rousseff directly, not first decide on whether accusations merited a trial.

For Cunha, there were advantages to doing it this way. The Senate was seen as more friendly, or at least less antagonistic toward Rousseff than the lower chamber. If senators had a chance to consider the legislation, they might simply throw it out.

With Rousseff directly facing trial, it would trigger her 180-day suspension from office — the time in which a trial was supposed to be conducted — putting Temer at least temporarily in power. For all Cunha's faults, he was a master political strategist. He surely figured that for the presidency, as is often said about property, possession would be a large step toward ownership.

Fachin was widely expected to block Cunha's fast-track impeachment plan. If it turned out that a majority of the other 10 justices were prepared to allow Cunha's plan, at the very least Fachin could stall. The longer it took, many Rousseff allies thought, the less likely her removal would become. After all, the political unrest was already causing problems in the economy, and on the horizon Brazil had the 2016 Summer Olympics, a time when the country would surely want to put its best foot forward.

Rules of Engagement

Even members of the Workers' Party who were not entirely opposed to the idea of getting rid of the unpopular bureaucrat-turned-president began reconsidering after Fachin was assigned the impeachment case. Ditching Rousseff to better position Lula for a comeback in 2018 was looking less likely. If Rousseff managed to end the impeachment proceedings at the Supreme Federal Tribunal, there would be only two roads for enemies and lukewarm allies to contemplate: Hope Brazil's electoral court removed both Rousseff and Temer for illegal campaign financing, as alleged in a lawsuit, or accept three more years of her administration and perhaps even help it function.

The campaign finance suit, filed by challenger Aécio Neves, alleged that the Rousseff-Temer ticket had gained an unfair advantage by getting illegal campaign contributions in 2014. The suit was initially thrown out in early 2015, but Neves appealed.

The suit was based on plea bargain testimony by Paulo Roberto Costa, the former Petrobras executive, who said that the Rousseff-Temer ticket had received money diverted from Petrobras oil contracts. This was part of the scheme being investigated in the Car Wash probe. The suit argued that the testimony was grounds to remove Rousseff and Temer and install Neves as president since he came in second place. PSDB also argued Rousseff abused her powers in having national addresses on TV during the campaign, manipulating economic indexes and using public buildings, chiefly the presidential residence, the Palácio da Alvorada, for political purposes.

The suit was complicated and had drawbacks even for Rousseff detractors. First, even if it could be proven that funds were illegally transferred, proving that Rousseff or Temer had knowledge would be much more difficult. Second, this kind of financing was common in Brazilian politics (this will be discussed in more depth later). Finally, the constitution says that the speaker of the Chamber of Deputies, in this case Cunha, would be the one to take over if the president and vice president were deposed.

That possibility made many wary.

All of that context was likely on the minds of the justices deciding on Cunha's fast-track proposal.

After all, the justices would also help decide the future of Cunha, who was dogged by accusations of corruption, obstruction of justice and influence peddling. For the beleaguered president, the embattled speaker was almost a favored antagonist, a foil to argue that the allegations against her were much less serious.

With Fachin as rapporteur, Cunha's allies also considered turning their backs on him. After all, who needs a troubled and unpopular speaker if he no longer has the power to trigger an impeachment proceeding against the president?

Cunha appeared unfazed. He clearly didn't believe Fachin's role would put his plans in jeopardy. Instead, he became even more driven to unseat Rousseff, in large part to try to save his own skin. Once the president was gone, Cunha allies openly hoped the speaker would be spared thanks to his services. And when he delivered, of course, it would be with the promise that he would not be stripped of his seat, as losing it would considerably increase his chance of going to jail.

"The government wants to shift media attention from the impeachment proceedings to me and the PMDB," said Cunha, speaking about the Car Wash probe, which now had him and his party in its sights.[14] Just days earlier, federal police had raided Cunha's residence and those of other PMDB leaders, the latest in the sprawling investigation. By this point, Cunha was facing several charges, including allegations that he took up to $40 million in bribes for him and allies in the Petrobras scheme, and had laundered money through an evangelical megachurch.

"Every day, there are images of the robbery led by the Workers' Party," Cunha continued. "And then all of a sudden there is a raid against the

---

14. Cunha was quoted by daily *Último Segundo* on Dec. 15, 2015.

PMDB? There is something strange in the air, but I am absolutely confident that there's no wrongdoing on our side."

Many Brasília insiders believed that Cunha would go down, regardless of what happened to Rousseff. There were just too many mounting allegations. On Dec. 16, 2015, Attorney General Rodrigo Janot requested that the Supreme Federal Tribunal remove Cunha from Congress so he couldn't tamper with the investigations against him. But nobody knew how long it would take the court to rule on that petition, and at the moment the full court was considering Cunha's pathway to impeachment.

Many Cunha allies feared an irreversible defeat could ultimately save the president and put the speaker closer to prison. After all, the 11 justices were not just expected to rule on Fachin's report and the shaky merits of the president's alleged fiscal crimes, budget maneuvering that other leaders had committed in recent Brazilian history. They would also be considering the country's stability and weighing the risks of giving so much power to a speaker who was clearly using his office to try to force out an unpopular president for actions that most Brazilians didn't fully understand.

Leaks of a decision, common in Brazil, did not happen this time with Fachin. Many took that as a sign that the court's rookie was determined to be discreet. When he began to explain his vote, the grounds of the Palácio do Planalto started shaking.

"The Senate does not have the authority to reject the authorization given by the Chamber of Deputies," said Fachin, clearly going with Cunha's pathway to impeachment.

In a nutshell, whatever the Chamber of Deputies decided would have to be tried by senators. Senators were less anti-Rousseff than deputies and the president had a close alliance with Senate President Renan Calheiros. But if Fachin's view prevailed, it was sure they would have to put the president on trial immediately, just as Cunha wanted.

That wasn't all. Fachin also rejected Rousseff's request to strip Cunha of the speakership, which had been argued on the grounds that as leader of the impeachment proceedings he was inherently biased. The justice countered that political disagreements are "natural and impartiality is not a remarkable characteristic of Congress."

Fachin also accepted a part of the pathway that exponentially increased the chance of an anti-Rousseff vote in the Chamber of Deputies: He kept Cunha's decision to form a special commission that would vote on the legislation before it was sent to the full Chamber of Deputies. That meant that the vote on impeachment in that phase could be secret, which would allow legislators to make an important decision without defending it to the people.

In short, Fachin ruled 100 percent against Rousseff. When his vote ended, several justices gasped. It would be for them to decide on the following day whether the impeachment fast track would go forward.

In the presidential palace, many Rousseff allies were distraught. Other supporters of the president, including Justice Minister José Eduardo Cardozo, still believed she could prevail, Fachin's decision notwithstanding.

Still, after that vote, the Rousseff administration's ability to survive was suddenly in doubt. "Impeachment rapporteur frustrates the government," said a headline in *Folha de S.Paulo*, the nation's largest daily newspaper.

Detractors of the president, both politicians and members of media companies who openly spoke against her, celebrated as if she could be removed within weeks. There was little talk about what her replacement, Temer, would be like, or how the move would put Cunha dangerously close to the presidency.

That night Rousseff met with some of her closest allies: Lula, chief of staff Jaques Wagner, Cardozo and Workers' Party president Rui Falcão. Despite the setback, Rousseff was confident.

"They won't accomplish anything attacking my biography," she said after the meeting. "I'm a woman who fought. I love my country and I'm honest.

"What's ironic is that many who want to cut my mandate short have a biography that wouldn't stand up to a quick Google search," she said, clearly speaking about Cunha.[15]

But even if Rousseff was a saint by comparison to Cunha, a kick-all-the-bums-out attitude was deepening on the streets in the later months of 2015.

"First, we remove Dilma. Then Cunha, Temer and all the other crooks," became one of the most often heard chants at protests.

Far-right protesters, sometimes led by Bolsonaro's sons Flávio, Eduardo and Carlos, also politicians, presented an even harsher approach, saying only military intervention could calm things down if Rousseff was not removed. This kind of rhetoric was common for the Bolsonaros, particularly the father, who often spoke in the superlative about the dictatorship and floated military options to problems. The difference was that those ideas were now becoming less fringe and more common amid the turmoil.

The day after Fachin voted, the court session resumed with a second vote from another Rousseff appointee. Justice Luís Roberto Barroso, formerly a law professor at Rio de Janeiro's state university, was never an open supporter of the president before being appointed in 2013. But his advocacy for human rights gave him fame and a soft spot in the hearts of Brazilian leftists and liberals.

Barroso often followed his colleagues' decisions, avoided sarcastic comments and was media shy. But a different Barroso showed up for that session. Elegant and sharp in explaining his decision, Barroso ruled almost entirely against Fachin on every aspect of Cunha's pathway. It was basically a pro-Rousseff vote, which in itself did not block Cunha's roadmap from going forward but did slow the proceedings.

---

15. Rousseff was quoted by state news agency *Agência Brasil* on Dec. 16, 2015.

Barroso criticized what he said was an attempt to short-circuit the Senate's role in evaluating an impeachment petition, saying it would be "unworthy for a body of constitutional stature to function as a rubber stamp" to what the Chamber of Deputies decided. Instead, he said the Senate should have the chance, by a simple majority vote, to decide whether to proceed with a trial. What's more, Rousseff would not be suspended until that vote happened, he ruled.

Barroso also blasted Cunha's attempt to allow the commission vote to be kept secret, saying the speaker's entire rationale boiled down to: "It will be secret because I want it to be."

"Life in democracy doesn't work like that," said Barroso.[16]

Now the remaining nine justices would have to pick: either keep Fachin's decision or go with Barroso's dissenting vote.

The next justice up was another Rousseff appointee, but how he would vote was a mystery. Teori Zavascki was considered the most unbiased on the court, and his vote would be listened to with special attention because he was also overseeing the prosecution of sitting officials in the growing Car Wash investigation.

Despite a few minor disagreements, Zavascki supported Barroso's separate vote. That surely made Rousseff's camp feel confident again since the next two justices had also been appointed by Rousseff.

One was Rosa Maria Weber, a specialist on labor issues who often agreed with Zavascki. The other was Luiz Fux, a justice and jujitsu black belt. Both voted with Barroso, against Fachin.

"Mystery, secrecy and democracy don't go together," said Fux as he voted, referring to Cunha's attempt to keep the commission vote secret.

The next justice to vote was a former attorney of the Workers' Party, appointed by Lula in 2009. José Dias Toffoli became the youngest justice

---

16. Barroso's vote, per the norm with Supreme Federal Tribunal hearings, was carried live on national television. *G1* published video clips of his decision.

ever appointed to the court at 41 years old. Soon after his appointment, fellow justices joked behind the scenes that he was "the new intern."

If he voted with Barroso, Rousseff would need just one more to stall Cunha and the impeachment plotters. But Toffoli voted 100 percent with Fachin. Toffoli criticized supporters of Barroso for trying to interfere in legislative matters. His comments had Workers' Party stalwarts wondering what happened to their one-time ally.

Toffoli's vote led many to speculate that Lula himself wanted Rousseff out of the picture so he could be the Workers' Party standard bearer in 2018, but that interpretation would be impossible to prove one way or another.

The next up was another Lula appointee, Cármen Lúcia, perhaps the most popular justice among Brazilians who follow matters related to the Supreme Federal Tribunal. In this conservative country, her approach was approvingly regarded as stereotypically feminine. For example, Lúcia sometimes used poetry in her decisions. The balanced and soft-spoken magistrate was once filmed baking cookies at her home in Brasília.

Saying very little, Lúcia quickly supported Barroso's decision in its entirety.

Rousseff, whose administration looked to be teetering on the edge only the day before, now only needed one more vote. Still, there was no way it would come from the justice up next.

Justice Gilmar Mendes had been appointed by President Fernando Henrique Cardoso, whose 1995-2002 presidency was marked by conservative policies that included a drive toward privatization and taming inflation by pegging the Brazilian real to the U.S. dollar.

Mendes, a sharp-tongued magistrate who spoke German, had served Cardoso as solicitor general. He was a deep thinker on the role of the top court and frequent critic of the Workers' Party and its leadership. He was also unpopular among many average Brazilians for releasing top political and business figures from prison. Two of his key positions were against judicial excesses and interference with legislative affairs.

In his vote against Rousseff, Mendes roared, making caustic remarks about Barroso's position. Ironically, his aggressive posture may have given Rousseff supporters some peace: Mendes' reaction was so loud in part because he probably knew that his side was about to be defeated.

And so it was in all the votes that followed.

Justice Marco Aurélio Mello, seen as the most unpredictable, went for Rousseff. Celso de Mello, the court's longest serving member, did the same. Finally, Chief Justice Ricardo Lewandowski, often criticized as being too favorable to requests of the Workers' Party, cast his vote in favor of Barroso's report.

Cunha's fast-track pathway to impeachment was defeated 8-3. The request to remove the speaker from office, however, was not accepted.

Even though Cunha would remain as speaker, administration officials were relieved. Rousseff aides believed that the ruling was a sign that the court would also annul any impeachment effort due to the flimsiness of the charges against Rousseff.

Cardozo, Rousseff's top lawyer in her impeachment defense, frequently said that if necessary he would repeatedly appeal to the country's top court to quash the rebellion. Cunha's efforts had clearly suffered a setback and the speaker knew it.

"Barroso intervened, stopped the impeachment process and, at that moment, gave Dilma a lifeline since it would be very easy for her to get a simple majority at the Senate to avoid being removed," Cunha would later say.[17] "As I knew that, I decided to wait for the end of the congressional recess, which was starting at that moment, to carry the process forward. A defeat was a likely hypothesis then."

Rousseff thought that result would, at least, give her a calm month of January to put her base back together and govern. She believed politicians who didn't like her could be charmed back into the ruling coalition,

---

17. Cunha made the comment in his 2021 book *Bye, Dear: A Diary of Impeachment*.

even if that was in exchange for government positions and the payment of earmarks to help her allies remain somewhat popular in 2016 mayoral elections nationwide. The key, she knew, would be to bring Temer and his PMDB party back into the fold. The party was clearly split by Cunha and the impeachment process.

Other smaller parties and some lawmakers, except for those gravitating around rightist figures like Bolsonaro, could also be used to govern if the PMDB did not heed the call. Though unpopular, Rousseff still had the power of the presidency at her disposal.

Some of Brazil's biggest media companies, and a big chunk of the population, were clearly against her and her Workers' Party. Still, Rousseff believed her Cabinet could weather the storm among politicians, her finance minister could pull the country out of a recession and her mentor, Lula, could keep part of the streets on her side.

If all of those failed, there was also the same Supreme Federal Tribunal that had ruled in her favor even after a former ally went against her.

"She is sure that she will win this battle," said Wagner, her chief of staff, after the court had voted. "I believe the court fulfilled a noble function of moderating the republic."[18]

18. Wagner was quoted in news magazine *Exame* in an article published Dec. 17, 2105.

CHAPTER 5

The Economy Sinks Further

A leaked research note by Banco Santander in the middle of the 2014 campaign had made public what market observers had known for months: Brazil's financial elite wanted Dilma Rousseff out. Their favorite for the presidential election was opposition leader Aécio Neves, a conservative and much more conciliatory politician. If that wasn't possible, they could work with environmentalist Marina Silva, who had members of the powerful Itaú bank family on her side.

Despite Rousseff's tax breaks to big companies and still high interest rates[19] to keep banks happy, Brazil's big money didn't want her interventionist micromanaging style. Her strained relationship with politicians across the spectrum was also palpable.

"If the president stabilizes or rises in polls, a scenario of a setback might appear" for the economy, Santander's research note to its wealthiest clients said.[20] "The exchange rate will devalue again, interest rates will rise and the stock market will fall, reversing part of the recent gains."

Rousseff allies became enraged by the bad omen presented by the Santander statement. The analyst who wrote it was fired soon after, but the message was clear. Even with a victory, the president would not have the support of many in the business community and she would struggle to do as she wanted to the economy.

With that backdrop, Rousseff began her second term in January 2015 with growing angst among foreign and national investors but with a strategy to deal with Brazil's faltering economy: Appoint a finance minister who was so pro-austerity and different from her that stock markets would stop betting against the president and confidence would return. But that plan, which began unraveling from the get-go, completely fell apart just days after the impeachment legislation was submitted.

When beleaguered Finance Minister Joaquim Levy resigned on Dec. 18, 2015, less than a year after he was put in as an economic game-changer, the brief statement that Rousseff put out had the usual appreciative language that always feels empty in such situations. But the single sentence thanking the man for his service included an exaggeration that went to the heart of her troubles.

---

19. Interest rates steadily climbed during Rousseff's time in office, and were 14 percent by 2016, according to Brazil's central bank.
20. Excerpts of the note were published by website *G1* on July 25, 2014.

"The president appreciates the dedication of Minister Joaquim Levy, who had a fundamental role in confronting the economic crisis, and wishes him success in future endeavors," said the statement. She had used warmer words for ministers who stepped aside due to corruption charges.

Rousseff had tapped Levy — nicknamed "Scissor Hands" thanks to his penchant for trimming budgets as head of the National Treasury under Lula — to help her government out of what was becoming an economic abyss. She chose him believing that austerity, while not the only path out of the crisis, would calm markets down and buy time.

Levy had been appointed with the backing of Luiz Trabuco, CEO of Levy's last employer, Bradesco, Brazil's biggest private bank. Lula was also reportedly supportive of the move.[21]

Rousseff had clearly figured that a man from banking would earn the trust of people like the Santander analyst who wrote the damaging note.

However, not only did Levy fail to "confront the economic crisis," but indications were that things had gotten worse in the year he spent trying. It wasn't entirely his fault, since the political rebellion against the president had exacerbated the economy's struggles. But when the person Rousseff had sent in to right the ship departed, the resignation laid bare her own failure — and it was two-fold.

Not only was she lacking a coherent plan for the growing crisis, but Levy's appointment and attempts at austerity had alienated many supporters. How had Rousseff, herself an economist by training, gotten to this point?

In 2010, when Rousseff was Lula's chief of staff and became a candidate for office for the first time in her life, Brazil's gross domestic product grew 7 percent. There was so much confidence in what had become the world's fifth largest economy that Lula felt emboldened to appoint

---

21. An article in daily *Folha de S.Paulo* on Nov. 21, 2014, reported on the support of various people for the appointment of Levy.

an untested politician to run for the highest job in the land.

Beyond the economic gains, Brazil had just secured the rights to host the 2016 Olympic Games in Rio de Janeiro. Brazil was also preparing to host the 2014 World Cup, the first time the soccer giant had done that since 1950. São Paulo was also bidding to host Expo 2020.

The discovery of huge deepwater oil reserves gave a boost to Brazilians' dreams of drastically improving education and health care and tackling the wide disparities in wealth and opportunity that made the country one of the most unequal in the world.

"It's being proved that God is Brazilian," Lula proclaimed in 2007 after the government announced the discovery of the vast offshore oil reserves.

Brazil wasn't just on the rise because of luck, however. A minimum-wage policy ended up allowing the poorest Brazilians to earn much more than even the US $100 a month that Lula had promised when he took over in 2003.

Brazil's minimum wage was created by populist President Getúlio Vargas in 1934, but wasn't fully implemented until the 1940s. It didn't cover all Brazilian workers because many were informally paid by their bosses. Shortcomings aside, the minimum wage was a national reference point, especially in poorer regions where earnings were much lower. Lula, who grew up poor and as a labor organizer spent years traveling around Brazil before becoming president, knew that.

When Lula took office, the minimum wage was US $75 monthly. Up to that point, the norm had been that in May of each year, the minimum wage would be adjusted to make up partially or totally for the rise of inflation the previous year. Only rarely did that adjustment translate into real gains.

In 2005, one year before Lula's run for reelection, his administration got a bill through Congress implementing a formula that took into account the percentage of GDP growth and inflation the two previous years plus. When Lula finished his second presidential term in 2010, the minimum wage was almost US $290. That gave his chosen successor candidate a massive electoral boost. As president, Rousseff kept the policy in place.

By 2015, the Brazilian real had devalued sharply against the U.S. dollar, lowering buying power because the prices of many products in Brazil are based on the dollar; in dollars, the minimum wage had shrunk to US $236 a month.

While the minimum wage helped the president maintain support in poorer areas of the country, it wasn't like before. Many supporters took it for granted, expecting new increases every year regardless of who was in office. Business leaders, however, wanted to put an end to the formula, enshrined in the law, that would grant raises to workers until 2019.[22]

Besides the minimum-wage policy, social programs literally ended famine in the country's most forgotten regions, according to the United Nations.

As Lula himself said, "The most needy are now in the federal budget."

The result: About 30 million people moved out of poverty between 2004 and 2014.[23] That was quite an achievement for a country that little more than a decade previously, under President Fernando Henrique Cardoso, had been celebrating the taming of rampant inflation.

During the glory days of the Workers' Party in the presidency, many economists saw a Brazilian miracle based on a consumption model. After all, people who had nothing could now buy televisions, refrigerators and cars. Government-sponsored housing boomed thanks to a new program, which also gave more jobs to builders and construction companies.

Brazil offered credit like never before. In December 2002, credit

---

22. Brazil's minimum wage in dollars going back to the 1990s was published by think tank DIEESE.

23. A World Bank article on millions leaving poverty in Brazil was last updated and published on Oct. 14, 2019.

corresponded to 26 percent of GDP. By December 2010, it was an astonishing 45.2 percent.[24] The feel-good factor was everywhere. Lula had both lifted millions out of poverty and allowed the rich to get richer.

The oil discoveries were the icing on the cake. Brazil could become the Latin American version of Saudi Arabia, with billions of barrels waiting to be exported to finance investment in education and healthcare.

"That's my man right there," U.S. President Barack Obama said while greeting Lula at the G-20 Summit in London in 2009. "The most popular politician on earth."

Lula became the most popular Brazilian president ever with a tripod of factors that supported economic growth: A commodities boom paid for more social inclusion, and that fostered internal consumption. But time proved that skeptics had very good reasons to criticize the consumption-based model.

Amid the glow of international acclaim, very few dared to note that structurally Brazil's economy was fundamentally the same. Interest rates were still high and hampered investment, little reform was enacted to make the country more competitive globally, and huge tax breaks to corporations didn't come with requirements for them to offer a certain amount of jobs or reinvest in the country.

Brazil's booming economy made Lula a poster boy for the world's moderate left. But soon after Rousseff took over, the first leg of the tripod broke: Commodity prices dropped sharply. The price of iron ore, one of Brazil's main exports, fell 80 percent from 2011 to the end of 2015.[25] A similar picture could be seen with oil, including the kind being extracted from the pre-salt layers; now that was too expensive to tap.

---

24. An analysis was done by economic institute Ipea (Instituto de Pesquisa Econômica Aplicada) and published in 2015.

25. Statistics on commodity prices were published in news magazine *Época Negócios* on Dec. 9, 2015.

When only a small crowd attended Rousseff's second inaugural cere-mony, Brazil's Central Bank predicted 0.69 percent growth in 2015. That was going to be hugely frustrating for a divided country that had given Rousseff such a tight reelection victory.

The disappointment was obvious to anyone following Brazil's figures. To make it worse, political analysts expected turmoil on the streets simi-lar to the mega-demonstrations of 2013. After all, Rousseff had promised no cuts. But that was going to be impossible for several reasons: Revenues were dropping, Rousseff's personality didn't jive with the back-slapping ways of Brasília, and the makeup of Congress was the most conservative in decades.

Financial institutions far from her base of supporters demanded aus-terity to put Brazil back on the growth path. Rousseff knew she couldn't ignore those demands. Even before the Santander memo leaked, every time she did well in polls during the 2014 campaign, the stock market went down.

Then there were the liabilities of her finance minister, Levy. Before joining Bradesco, he had had a long stint coordinating the Rio de Janeiro state government's finances. At the time, Rio was seen as a great example nationwide. It would take years and the massive Car Wash investigation to show that the optimism was not justified.

Despite Levy's personal credentials as a loyal and serious worker for two presidents, Lula and Cardoso, in early 2015 he was disliked by every-one in politics. The left said he had no creativity, knew nothing but cut-ting expenses and behaved like an errand boy of financial markets. The right thought he had no authority to enforce austerity and that he was being used by an unreliable president to buy time.

Besides, in the course of 2015 the finance minister developed a nem-esis: Budget minister Nelson Barbosa, also an economist and a former student of the New School of New York, an antagonist of the neolib-eral thinking spread worldwide by alumni of the University of Chicago, such as Levy. Much closer to Rousseff's Workers' Party, Barbosa steadily undermined Levy's positions on cuts.

Their spats spilled into public view, and sometimes were even absurd. In May 2015, after a meeting with the vice president Levy announced that the government would look to cut between 70 and 80 billion reals (between US $23.3 billion and US $26.6 billion at the time) from the budget.[26]

Barbosa lobbied hard with allies in the Cabinet, eventually persuading Rousseff to propose cuts under the 70 billion reals mark. The number announced? 69.9 billion reals.[27]

Even though the difference was relatively small, on the afternoon of May 22, 2015, the two men were to give a press conference about the budget trimming. Levy, outmaneuvered and fuming according to press reports, didn't show up. The reason his office gave: He had the flu.[28]

One year after Levy and Barbosa took office, one question was a constant for them: Who was staying and who was going? Whoever stayed wasn't going to call it a win, though. Due to the uncertainties in the economy and the political crisis, the projection of a 0.69 percent increase in GDP turned out to be painfully wrong. In fact, the economy suffered the biggest fall in more than two decades: a contraction of 3.8 percent.[29]

The last straw for Scissor Hands came when Rousseff decided to ignore his advice on how much Brazil should save to service debt in 2016. Levy wanted 0.7 percent of the country's GDP reserved for debt, called

---

26. Levy was quoted in magazine *Veja* on May 18, 2015.

27. Announcement of the budget cut number was published by news website *G1* May 22, 2015.

28. Daily *O Globo* published the reason Levy's office gave for his absence on May 22, 2015.

29. News website *G1* published an article on the economy's contraction on March 3, 2016.

the "primary surplus," but the president went with just 0.5 percent. That might seem like a minor detail, but for Levy it was yet another way he was being discredited.

The primary surplus had been one of three major elements of Brazil's macroeconomic policy since Cardoso's presidency. The others were a floating exchange rate and inflation targets. Rousseff was interfering in all three.

Brazil's central bank frequently bought and sold dollars to handle the exchange rate market, and inflation was rising to more than 10 percent. The president believed a little currency manipulation and higher prices would not affect the broad economy, and at some point, when growth returned, those two items would not make a huge difference. The financial markets disagreed.

Rousseff's determination of a primary surplus smaller than her finance minister recommended became the tipping point for Levy. With less money to service debt, the crisis of confidence would deepen. After all, the same administration had predicted a budget deficit of about US $10 billion for the following year.

"I feel a little obfuscated," Levy said one day before leaving.[30]

That reportedly prompted Lula to talk to Rousseff about appointing Henrique Meirelles, who had been a successful conservative central bank governor for eight years.[31] But Rousseff didn't trust Meirelles. The rivalry they developed during the Lula years had become too strong for her to accept him as her finance minister. Meirelles himself wasn't excited about working with a president who had frequently undermined him and whose poor management of the economy was partially to blame for a drop in Brazil's investment grade from all rating agencies.

---

30. Levy was quoted by news portal *G1* on Dec. 16, 2015.
31. Among others, Lula's suggestion about taking Meirelles on was reported by daily *Estadão* on Nov. 11, 2015.

The Economy Sinks Further

In the end, Barbosa took over.

His appointment showed that Rousseff trusted him, but it was also a sign that her bonds with the financial sector were completely broken. After one year trying to gain confidence among brokers and bankers, Rousseff appeared to be giving up.

By then she had lost much of her base, Brazil's economy was in deep trouble and the country's elite were looking at alternatives.

CHAPTER 6

Spin Doctor Jailed

Even as Congress was beginning to take up the impeachment legislation in early 2016, Rousseff was confident she would prevail.

First, the Supreme Federal Tribunal had rejected Cunha's attempt to fast-track the process. That meant that two-thirds of the Chamber of Deputies would have to vote in favor for the petition to move it to the Senate, where a simple majority would then have to vote on whether to suspend the president while a trial took place within 180 days to decide on final removal. Those steps would give her administration time to change the narrative, and the more time that passed the more Cunha's legal troubles mounted. If he was arrested, the entire impeachment process could be thrown into question.

Second, her administration could continue to fight her detractors' narrative that she had done something gravely wrong. The two central accusations in the impeachment petition were: She had issued decrees to authorize borrowing for social programs without Congress' approval and her administration had ordered state banks to distribute money for government programs instead of having that spending originate from the National Treasury, the so-called "fiscal maneuvering." The sum of these actions, impeachment proponents claimed, was that Rousseff employed accounting tricks to shore up support and mask yawning deficits as revenue dropped sharply.

Rousseff's administration argued the decrees were not done in malice but rather to provide budget flexibility, and that a bill was submitted to adjust revenue targets.

With regard to fiscal maneuvering, Rousseff often noted that former presidents had done similar things and faced no consequences. If such budget maneuvering was a crime, then previous administrations should have been thrown out, Rousseff would argue. As the fact-checking organization Aos Fatos reported, Rousseff had a point, as such manipulation had happened under predecessors Luiz Inácio Lula da Silva and Fernando Henrique Cardoso.

But that wasn't the whole story. Analyzing government spending ledgers, Aos Fatos found that the total amount of money moved in such operations under Rousseff was 35 times the total of that during the administrations of Lula and Cardoso combined (33 billion reals versus 933 million).[32] What's more, in 2014 alone, Rousseff's administration had done eight such operations, compared to three by Lula and

32. Fact-checking website Aos Fatos published its findings on April 16, 2016.

four by Cardoso over the eight years that each was in office.

"Exaggerated," Aos Fatos rated Rousseff's claim that her administration had done the same thing as previous governments.

Still, there were other considerations. Some of those operations had taken place in 2011 and 2012, when Brazil's economy was still booming. That made it harder for opponents to make a convincing case that in those instances Rousseff's administration had been trying to mask problems or garner support for a reelection bid still a few years away. And in 2014, Brazil's economy was beginning to crash. Had the government not gotten a little creative, it stands to reason that at the very least, payments for programs for the poor, a lifeline for many, would have been delayed.

Those things could and would be explained, administration officials reasoned. What's more, the final impeachment legislation put before Congress was limited to alleged infractions in Rousseff's current term, which began in 2015. In sum, Rousseff's legal team was confident a strong defense could be mounted.

Rousseff's bigger challenge was to distance herself from key members of her party getting into trouble. So far, none of the people jailed for corruption were in her inner circle. They had all been appointed by former presidents Cardoso and Lula. That made it more difficult to galvanize support against her.

After a calm January, the embattled leader appeared to be so confident of political survival that in early February she took her family to the northeastern state of Bahia for a beach vacation during Carnival. One week later, her inner circle was breached.

João Santana hadn't even spent his first night in jail before the battle lines were being drawn. The marketing expert and his wife, Mônica Moura, were arrested Feb. 23, 2016, on the orders of Car Wash judge Sergio Moro. According to the indictment, the pair allegedly used secret foreign bank accounts to receive millions of dollars in illicit funds from offshore companies controlled by Odebrecht, one of the major Brazilian construction companies implicated in the scandal.

Santana wasn't just one more marketing specialist; He had overseen Lula's successful 2006 re-election campaign and then Rousseff's 2010 and 2014 bids, successes that brought him folk hero status within the ranks of the Workers' Party. He was credited as being one of the first to introduce U.S.-style political strategies that included gathering large amounts of data on the electorate and using focus groups to hone messages.

To Rousseff, the Santanas were more than just employees. They were her friends, advisors in difficult moments, both political and personal. The Santanas had advised Rousseff to reveal she had a treatable lymphoma shortly before the 2010 presidential election. The Santanas also told Rousseff she should be more combative toward adversaries in the 2014 race, which led her to burn many bridges with the opposition but got her re-elected despite many challenges. Their bond finally broke when Mônica said in plea bargain testimony that Rousseff had warned them that their arrest was imminent, which Rousseff always denied.

When the couple went down, Rousseff and the Workers' Party tried to distance themselves. The opposition, though, came forward with another major reason to remove the president: The Santanas and Rousseff were closely connected. It didn't matter that the couple couldn't even be remotely tied to the impeachment petition against Rousseff. What mattered, opposition leaders argued, was the close association.

The arrest of the Santanas also gave the opposition extra ammunition in case impeachment failed. Their arrest dovetailed with the alleged illegal campaign finances of the Rousseff-Temer ticket being considered by the Superior Electoral Tribunal. If the court ruled against Rousseff and Temer, the ticket would be annulled.

"It's clear that the bribe scheme . . . fueled the campaign," said Rubens Bueno, a deputy from the Popular Socialist Party. "Even the Workers' Party guru of lies can't escape Car Wash."

Aécio Neves added his voice, saying that the accusations were "the most serious yet" in the corruption scandal and would be included in his party's case against Rousseff at the electoral court.

Rousseff supporters said that all the payments to Santana had been declared, and that the president had no connection to what Moro was alleging.

"We repudiate, with vehemence, the attempt by sectors of the opposition, without any elements (of proof), to associate the investigation and the precautionary measures by the federal justice system to the publicist João Santana and the electoral campaign of President Dilma Rousseff," said Flávio Caetano, lawyer for Rousseff's 2014 campaign.

According to Moro, the scheme worked like this: For his services, at the behest of the Workers' Party, Santana was paid $7.5 million via a shell company connected to Odebrecht, money that originally came from state oil company Petrobras. Santana then allegedly "washed" that money by buying several properties.

How much the Rousseff-Temer campaign benefited from those payments, or other forms of illegal financing, would be impossible to measure. And neither president nor vice president was accused of personal gain, but that didn't mean the administration could avoid getting stained.

In Brazil, illegal campaign financing has a special name: Cash Register 2, universally known as "Caixa 2." It works by channeling funds to political parties via overpriced contracts, evaded taxes, services paid for but never rendered and many other ways that Brazilian creativity allows.

Brazilian and foreign companies need government contracts. To lobby for those contracts, they fundraise for candidates. But taking a stand in a presidential election can really hurt business if a company ends up betting on the wrong horse. So, through the 2014 election (the rules have since been changed), businesses legally donated across the political spectrum and then gave even more illegally to candidates they favored.

Businesses gave money to candidates and parties in many ways. One of the most common ways was to transfer funds to offshore bank accounts, without informing electoral authorities, and then channel that money to candidates back in Brazil. Another common way was to divert funds from inflated public contracts, or pay for social media expenses not clearly linked to a specific candidate.

Through the 2014 elections, all political parties that produced a presidential winner had taken advantage of that corrupt system. However, it spilled out into public view in new ways during the Workers' Party administrations — despite the fact that party leaders had preached against Caixa 2 throughout their careers. Neves and his PSDB, as much as Temer and his PMDB, were also caught. But it was the president's party that won elections promising to govern in a more ethical manner, and it clearly hadn't done that.

The rise of the Santanas paralleled the increasing importance of Caixa 2. Their mentor, Duda Mendonça, one of the most successful spin-doctors in Latin American history, oversaw Lula's successful 2002 campaign. He would have likely also worked on Lula's 2006 campaign, but he got caught up in a major corruption scandal that roiled the Workers' Party. Under pressure, in 2005 Mendonça testified in Congress that he was paid by the Workers' Party via an offshore bank account.

Mendonça would stop working with the Workers' Party, but the damage was done: The party that had made criticizing Caixa 2 a central part of its platform was also using it.

Former Minister Ciro Gomes, one of Lula's closest allies before the two grew apart, often used a colorful phrase to describe the general disappointment of average Brazilians at that moment.

"People accept that the faithful can be sinners, but not the priest," he said.[33]

The system of Caixa 2, which would develop over decades, was connected to construction companies like Odebrecht, which had been involved in Brazilian politics since its founding in the 1940s.

Started by a German family in the southern state of Santa Catarina, the company flourished and grew in the Northeastern state of Bahia. And that rise happened with help from Petrobras, which was founded in 1953.

At that time, Caixa 2 was not needed; bribes were enough to keep the system running. Historian Pedro Henrique Campos, an expert on Odebrecht's history, says the company developed tight connections with the oil giant thanks to its first chairman, Juracy Magalhães, a military man from Bahia.

During Brazil's 1964-1985 military rule, Petrobras' military connections paid off. All the company needed to do was focus lobbying efforts on executives and government agencies. Much money was spent to gain government favor, and the practice was considered a good investment.

By the time democracy returned in 1985, Odebrecht had risen from one of the 20 largest construction companies in Brazil to one of the top three, according to Campos. Not bad for a business that was headquartered far from the financial heart of São Paulo. But to keep its status in the new era of Brazilian politics, the company added political parties and many individual lawmakers to its payroll. So did many of the other big companies. Caixa 2 was born.

From the time Mendonça offered testimony against the Workers' Party in 2005, Caixa 2 had been less tolerated in Brazilian political culture. And when the Santanas were arrested because of illegal Odebrecht money, Rousseff was surrounded by the vicious circle of Brazilian politics.

---

33. Among many other times, Gomes was quoted saying this by website *Conversa Afiada* on July 28, 2016.

The high road was not available for Rousseff and her party: Her campaign was no different from all the others that were fueled by dirty money. The best defense the Workers' Party had was to say Caixa 2 was not equivalent to bribes.

Rousseff's justice minister, José Eduardo Cardozo, one of the most eloquent in her inner circle, made an impassioned defense a few weeks after the Santanas were arrested. But it was hardly an argument that would inspire Rousseff supporters to take to the streets in support.

"There wasn't any kind of parallel fundraising. All I saw and witnessed does not indicate there was illegal campaign financing," said Cardozo.[34]

---

34. Cardozo was quoted by daily *Valor Economico* on Feb. 12, 2016.

CHAPTER 7

The Whip

It was an "earthquake," a development that could tarnish Rousseff, declared one of Brazil's top news anchors. No, it was simply a "gathering of lies," countered Rousseff's top lawyer.

No matter what the truth was, a leaked plea bargain reported in early March 2016 had deep impact — in part because the person delivering the allegations in the document had long been a Rousseff ally.

In November 2015, weeks before House Speaker Eduardo Cunha would take up impeachment legislation, Sen. Delcídio do Amaral, Rousseff's leader in the Senate, was arrested for an alleged attempt to interfere with the Car Wash investigation after he was recorded offering a former Petrobras director a way to leave the country before signing a plea bargain deal. Evidence against Amaral was so clear-cut that justices on the Supreme Federal Tribunal and his fellow senators agreed he deserved to be jailed.

Rousseff didn't speak about the arrest for two weeks. During a visit to Paris, she told reporters she had been surprised by Amaral's arrest but did not fear any revelations that the senator might make, as local media were reporting could happen. To hear Rousseff tell it, Amaral had simply gone astray.

"I am perplexed because I never thought this could happen with Sen. Delcídio," said Rousseff.[35]

Days later, with the impeachment process opened by speaker Cunha, Amaral was suspended from the Workers' Party for 60 days due to the allegations. According to unsourced news reports that began emerging, Amaral was feeling abandoned by the party. For Brasília insiders, that was understood as a threat—if Amaral didn't get help, he might talk. However, Rousseff's administration made no moves to try to get him out of jail.

When Amaral was sent to home arrest in the middle of February, top members of his Workers' Party, including those who sanctioned him in early December, feared a potential bombshell.

Their worries materialized when they went to newsstands on March 3, 2016, and saw the cover of *IstoÉ* weekly magazine.

"Delcídio tells everything," was the headline.

---

35. Globo's Jornal Nacional carried Rousseff's comments on Nov. 30, 2015, from Paris.

Amaral had apparently reached a plea bargain with authorities, and *IstoÉ* claimed to have obtained a leaked copy. The agreement had yet to be validated by Brazil's top court, a key part of the process, but regardless, the details were scintillating.

Among Amaral's claims were two directed at Rousseff. First, Amaral said the president was trying to interfere in the Car Wash probe. Second, he accused her of agreeing that Petrobras should buy a refinery in Pasadena, Texas, for US $1 billion during her days as Lula's chief of staff despite several warnings against the purchase from a government watchdog. The senator said the purchase was overpriced so that funds could be channeled as kickbacks for officials.

Rousseff, who was striking a more aggressive tone with adversaries, could surely deny the allegations, and she did forcefully. But she could not simply call her former advisor a coup monger or opposition figure with an axe to grind. Amaral had been part of the inner circle of her presidency. And his claims had added weight because of his access at Petrobras for more than a decade.

Appointed by then President Fernando Henrique Cardoso, Amaral was Petrobras' director for oil and gas between 1999 and 2001. He left the post after deciding to affiliate with the Workers' Party ahead of a run for governor in his home state of Mato Grosso do Sul. His decision was not prompted by leftist politics but rather by noticing a change was imminent in Brasília, according to friend and consultant at the time, Mario Rosa.[36] And that calculation was right: Lula beat Cardoso's candidate José Serra the following year to win the presidency.

Instead of running for governor, Amaral ran for senator in 2002 and won. That would change his career dramatically. Less than three years later, in the biggest crisis of the Lula presidency, he was picked to chair

---

36. Rosa recounts the decision-making process in his 2017 book, *Glory and Shame: Memories of a Crisis Consultor.*

the congressional inquiry commission for the "Mensalão" scandal of alleged kickbacks for political support. Many in the opposition praised his moderation and diligence, while other members of the Workers' Party pressured him to show his affiliation actually meant he was willing to keep their president in office. Suspicion that Amaral was not a loyal party man dogged him for many years.

After Lula won reelection in 2006, Amaral was relegated to a back seat in the Senate and was not considered for ministerial positions, signs that there was little fondness for him among administration insiders. Still, Amaral did not leave the ruling party.

When Rousseff took office in 2011, another chance to rise in the ranks knocked on the senator's door. Both he and the president were specialists in energy, and both were seen as untarnished politicians who took the fight against corruption very seriously. Those affinities with Rousseff helped him gain the role of government whip in the Senate, meaning he oversaw the parties that formed the governing coalition.

But now, despite being a close ally of Rousseff, the prospect of jail time and a looming vote in the Senate to remove Amaral from his seat had likely made him eager to sign a plea bargain just a few months after being arrested.

IstoÉ, like most of the editorial boards of Brazil's media at this point, made clear that it backed Rousseff's ouster.

"What's left but for her to leave?" said a cover story in December 2015.

A lengthy opinion piece in that same issue made the case that Rousseff should go.

"For the country, (impeachment) represents a light at the end of the tunnel of crisis, an opportunity to construct a national union that reverses expectations and regains credibility."[37]

---

37. The opinion piece was published in the Dec. 4, 2015 issue of IstoÉ.

So it was no surprise when the *IstoÉ* issue with the plea bargain scoop bestowed on Amaral total credibility even though the agreement had yet to be reviewed and approved by the Supreme Federal Tribunal.

"With an extraordinary richness of detail," said the second paragraph of the report, "the senator described the decisive action of President Dilma Rousseff to keep at the state-run company the directors involved in the corruption scheme and showed that, from the presidential palace, she used her powers to avoid the punishment for the corrupt and the corrupted, as she named a top court judge sure to vote for the release of construction executives already charged by Car Wash.[38]

"Sen. Delcídio also said former President Luiz Inácio Lula da Silva had full knowledge of the bribes paid at Petrobras and acted directly and personally to stop investigations — that includes ordering the payment of hush money to witnesses."

According to the article, Amaral told investigators that Rousseff privately asked him to talk to newly appointed Judge Marcelo Navarro of the Superior Tribunal of Justice, one of the country's top courts, about releasing from prison Odebrecht CEO Marcelo Odebrecht and his counterpart at the construction firm Andrade Gutierrez, Otávio Marques de Azevedo. Navarro had indeed voted to free the two executives, but four other judges on the court disagreed.

Navarro denied Amaral's accusations. In a statement, he said that meetings with lawmakers were a chance for him to introduce himself and talk about his professional experience.

"I never committed myself to anything" in order to be nominated, he said.[39]

The reach of *IstoÉ*, decades earlier a top news magazine, was fairly

---

38. The report on the plea bargain was published by news magazine *IstoÉ* on March 3, 2016.

39. *Folha de S.Paulo* reported Navarro's statement on March 3, 2016.

limited, as was its record of scoops in recent years. Still, the content of the plea bargain soon touched major TV networks that also portrayed Amaral's narrative as trustworthy.

TV Globo's Jornal Nacional, the one news program that reaches every corner of the country, opened its broadcast with anchor Renata Vasconcelos recounting the news in a dramatic tone.

"Brazilian politics suffered an earthquake today due to the revelation of the content of Sen. Delcídio do Amaral's testimony to federal prosecutors in a plea bargain deal," she said.[40] "Among other things, the suspended senator of the Workers' Party accused President Dilma and former President Lula of trying to interfere in the Car Wash probe."

The plea bargain reported by IstoÉ took 26 minutes of TV Globo's main news program, more than half of it. Beyond the main allegations, Jornal Nacional reported Amaral's comments on multiple events he said he witnessed dating back more than 10 years, including several suggesting that during his presidency Lula had used his office to protect friends and a son caught up in investigations, avoided his own impeachment after secretive negotiations with congressmen plus a myriad of other claims that were hard to verify but had weight because they came from a senator deeply entrenched in government business. No other witnesses supported Amaral's claims, however.

Scheduled for the same day the plea bargain story came out, Rousseff had a significant government move planned. José Eduardo Cardozo, one of her closest allies, was leaving as justice minister to take over as solicitor general. The change was necessary so Cardozo would be permitted by Congress to speak on behalf of the president during the upcoming impeachment proceedings. Cardozo was named several times in Amaral's plea, always as somebody who allegedly knew what was going on and supported Rousseff and Lula.

---

40. Jornal Nacional made the broadcast on March 3, 2016.

Looking calm and dressed in a sober white suit for the ceremony in Brasília, Rousseff did not mention Amaral by name in her remarks, but showed she was keen to carry on.

"We will continue to defend that the presumption of innocence cannot be replaced by the presumption of guilt," Rousseff said. "We shouldn't give place to widespread loathing without any formal accusation or to condemnation without due process due to illegal and selective leaks."

A long Cabinet meeting followed the ceremony, with Rousseff telling some of her main ministers to talk to reporters about Amaral's alleged desire for vengeance. Chief of Staff Jaques Wagner was one of the first to speak.

"Has anyone seen any evidence of what he says? I only saw statements in which he is the accuser, he is the witness, he is everything," Wagner said at a news conference in Brasília. "I don't think there is much substance there."

Solicitor General Cardozo, in his first press conference in the new job, said he was not sure whether the plea bargain testimony existed, since it had not been validated by judicial authorities. He also portrayed Amaral as a desperate man looking for a way out of trouble.

"Sen. Delcídio was very unhappy about being arrested. And very unhappy because he thought the administration should have acted to release him," Cardozo said. "If this testimony took place, it is a gathering of lies."

Cardozo also questioned Amaral's claims that Rousseff had interfered with the appointment of Judge Navarro so executives could be freed. Cardozo said the court where Navarro sits had another 13 judges named by the president. "If our administration had such behavior . . . defendants who we don't want in jail wouldn't be there now," he said. "And that court has not released anyone."

Rui Falcão, the Workers' Party chairman, a former journalist who understood how repercussions could dent the party, also spoke about Amaral.

"He has no credibility. President Lula didn't do the negotiations like he says nor did President Dilma interfere in appointments," Falcão told journalists at the Workers' Party headquarters in São Paulo. "I want to remind you that Delcídio has been suspended from the Workers' Party. So at this moment he is not affiliated with the Workers' Party and doesn't act as a senator of the party."

The opposition seized the opportunity, clearly figuring that adding to Rousseff's problems could only help bolster the case that she needed to go. Sen. Aécio Neves said Amaral's claims should be included in the ongoing impeachment proceedings against Rousseff, even though the impeachment accusations had nothing to do with anything Amaral alleged.

"It would be an unforgivable omission" if the impeachment commission and Chamber of Deputies were not able to consider the accusations, he told reporters in Brasília.

Congressman Pauderney Avelino, leader of the right-leaning DEM party in the lower house, also told reporters that Amaral's claims "brought Car Wash inside the presidential palace, to Dilma's lap."

"I compare this plea bargain to the one that brought former President Collor to impeachment," Avelino said. Collor's presidency began to crumble in 1992 after corruption allegations from his own brother Pedro were published in *Veja* magazine.

Facing removal proceedings himself, speaker Cunha struck a more moderate tone, without losing sight of the case he led to remove Rousseff.

"These are serious allegations, but they come from a plea bargain; they need to be verified," he told reporters in Brasília. "I just find it funny that the Workers' Party is now saying this comes from a plea bargain, but when it involves other people they have no problem with making accusations."

Another Rousseff adversary also celebrated the repercussions of Amaral's plea bargain, seeing the president closer to impeachment.

The São Paulo stock exchange, which had bet against her since the 2014 campaign, jumped 5.12 percent on that day. Petrobras stocks soared 16.3 percent even though the accusations put the company in a bad light; the bottom line even for Petrobras stocks was that Rousseff was closer to being removed.

All the president could do by the end of that tumultuous day was to put out another statement. Rousseff noted that the agreement had not been validated by the Supreme Federal Tribunal and lamented the leaks, saying they could destabilize the nation.[41] Amaral also issued a statement in which he neither confirmed nor denied the content of the reporting, but rather said he had not been contacted by the magazine.

If Amaral's allegations did not lead investigators to evidence, he would lose potential benefits of the plea, such as a commuted sentence and house arrest. But for Rousseff, it wouldn't really matter what happened in the future: Even if Amaral ended up discredited, the political damage was done.

"Delcidio's plea bargain leak came at a very bad time," Cardozo said in an interview, adding he felt personally betrayed by Amaral, who had been a friend.

"It was a new year, we were hoping for some calm to fight against the impeachment process," he commented. Instead, the news ended up being "a massacre in the media," he said. "We couldn't be heard at all."

---

41. News portal *G1* published Rousseff's statement on March 3, 2016.

CHAPTER 8

Mentor in Trouble

It was called "Operation Aletheia," the 24th raid in the ever-growing Car Wash investigation. The previous night, rumors of a major operation had been flying in journalism circles. Hours before any big raid was about to happen most reporters knew. And in this case, they also knew the remarkable targets: former President Luiz Inácio Lula da Silva and his family.

When police knocked on the door of Lula's home around 6 a.m. on March 4, 2016, he was awake and dressed. Early morning Car Wash raids had become standard fare in the country, and so it's likely Lula was not greatly surprised as Operation Aletheia unfolded.

For months, average Brazilians had been expecting it, too. Still, when word spread that morning, the biggest question in Brazil was: Would Lula be jailed?

As if in answer, the man who had left office at the end of 2010 with off-the-charts approval rating made clear he wasn't simply going to walk off with police. Far be it from such a dominating politician to let a good drama go to waste.

"Unless he was handcuffed" and forced out, Lula said he was not leaving his apartment in São Bernardo do Campo, a modest city in the outskirts of São Paulo, according to the report by police investigator Luciano Flores de Lima that was released two days later. De Lima said Lula told him he would only answer questions at his apartment.[42]

Judge Sergio Moro had ordered a judicial summons to force Lula to answer investigators' questions while essentially in custody — even if his legal team opposed such questioning. "Condução coercitiva," as it's called in Portuguese, is a part of the Brazilian penal code that allows judges to force suspects, witnesses, victims of a crime and others to answer questions without necessarily arresting or formally charging them.

Condução coercitiva made Car Wash very popular among average Brazilians, who saw it as a way to keep corrupt politicians and other elite from stalling investigations by constantly finding ways out of testifying. But the controversial mechanism also worried legal experts about excesses, especially when the target of the procedure, such as a former president, had not previously refused to give testimony.

Police did not want Lula to testify in his house. De Lima, the investigator, told Lula that eventually the news would get out and "protests and violent acts could happen around the property." So instead, police had set up for Lula's testimony in the Presidential Hall annex next to Congonhas Airport in São Paulo, over an hour away. Lula may well have thought

---

42. The account was published by Globo's Fantástico program on March 6, 2016.

what many supporters were thinking: Why take him to an airport — not the police headquarters in São Paulo — unless the plan was really to send him to Curitiba, the center of the Car Wash investigation where many of the country's elite had already been jailed?

Minutes after police knocked on Lula's door, union leaders and Workers' Party members throughout Brazil were grabbing their red shirts and heading to the streets. Pro-impeachment activists were energized, too. They believed that justice was finally coming to the Workers' Party and its leader.

After speaking with lawyer Roberto Teixeira, Lula told police he would change clothes and go with them. On Moro's orders, Lula was to travel in an unmarked car in the middle of the backseat, so as not to be seen. Lula, however, clearly wanted it all to be as public as possible. That's when he insisted on being handcuffed, according to de Lima.[43] A star on the political stage for decades, Lula saw an opportunity to play the victim.

In those first hours, confusion reigned. Was Lula being charged? Had he been arrested? Would he be jailed? The initial stories of many news organizations, both Brazilian and foreign, said Lula had been arrested or taken into custody. A statement by Moro clarified the situation.

"These investigative measures aim only to clarify the truth and do not mean an anticipation of guilt by the former president," Moro wrote.

The name of the operation, Aletheia, derived from the Greek word that means "pursuit of truth." Many Car Wash operations were given code names that were shared with the press on the days they launched. Most had a message, or referred to some aspect of the people and alleged crimes being investigated.

"Operation Final Judgement" involved the arrest on corruption charges of dozens of presidents and directors at more than a dozen engineering, gas and construction companies. "Operation Radioactivity" was

---

43. The report was recounted by daily Globo program *Bom Dia Brasil* on March 7, 2016.

81

the name given when executives of energy companies were arrested for alleged price-fixing for a nuclear project. And "Operation Erga Omnes," Latin meaning "valid for all," was the name given when leaders of construction companies Odebrecht and Andrade Gutierrez were arrested.

This time the operation was focused on Lula. Investigators asked questions related to several cases of alleged corruption by the former president, many of which originated in plea bargain deals with corporate executives and former political allies.

One case, discovered by daily *Folha de S.Paulo* that prosecutors then followed, identified Lula as the secret owner of a country house on the outskirts of São Paulo. Investigators believed the property and renovations sponsored by the construction company Odebrecht were actually favors in exchange for political benefit. Lula had gone to the country house, which on paper belonged to a friend of his, more than 100 times after the end of his presidency, investigators said.

Another case accused Lula of being promised by constructor OAS a beachfront apartment in the city of Guarujá, in the south of São Paulo state. Prosecutors' complex narrative said the former president was expected to receive more than US $1 million as compensation for three contracts between OAS and Petrobras. That payment was allegedly to be split between the purchase itself, which never went forward, and the renovations.

Investigators also said they were looking into 30 million Brazilian reais (US $8.12 million at the time) in payments for speeches and in donations to the Lula Institute by construction firms that were central players in the corruption scheme happening at Petrobras. For Workers' Party opponents, any eventual conviction would deliver a mighty blow: It could land Lula in jail and nix his chances of running in the 2018 elections.

As he often did as a candidate when attacked, Lula responded with humor during the interrogation, early on offering his lawyers some cheese bread that investigators had offered him.

During hours of testimony, later released by the Workers' Party, Lula interjected stories between denials that he had anything to do with the apartment in Guarujá, the questionable donations to the Lula Institute and other cases he was asked about.

Lula told investigators how during his first trip to the United Nations as president, in 2003, his security detail brought with them a popular chicken dish. When they got to the Waldorf Astoria hotel in New York, where Lula would be staying, the men thought that the safe in the room was a microwave. According to Lula, the men put the plate of food inside and closed the door.

"Then they couldn't get the safe open," Lula told the investigators. "I bet that chicken is still there today."[44]

Police questions about donations to the Lula institute and Lula's answers went around in an endless loop, with the former president repeatedly saying he didn't know.

Police investigator: "What was the annual average amount (of donations)?"

Lula: "Ah, I don't know. Don't ask me those things because I'm not the one who takes care of that."

Police investigator: "I see. You don't have any idea of how much . . ."

Lula: "Not in the institute nor in my house am I the one to take care of that. At home, there is a woman named Mrs. Marisa (his wife) who takes care of that and in the institute there are people who take care of that."

Police investigator: "You, sir, have no idea?"

Lula: "I have no idea."

Police investigator: "How much money comes in?"

---

44. Lula's story about the chicken was recounted in daily *Estadão* on March 14, 2016.

Lula: "And I insist I have no idea."[45]

Lula was combative in responding to questions about the Guarujá apartment, the case that investigators said was furthest along. When asked for details, dozens of times his answer was: "It's there," referring to documents that his legal team had previously provided. He argued that prosecutors should be the ones on trial because they had to prove the allegations since he never owned the apartment in question.

"I think I'm participating in the most complex case in the judicial history of Brazil," said Lula, surely in the sarcastic tone he often took when talking about the apartment. "I have an apartment that isn't mine, that I didn't pay for, I'm wanting to receive money that I paid, that a prosecutor says is mine, that the magazine *Veja* says is mine, that *Folha* (the daily paper) says is mine, and the federal police invents a dirty Homeric trick, invents a story about the apartment, invents a story about an offshore company in Panama that comes here, that had sold the place, a total story to connect me to Car Wash."

Rousseff was informed about Lula's questioning early on by Solicitor General José Eduardo Cardozo, who until recently as justice minister had been in charge of the federal police. Cardozo was never one of Lula's favorite allies. Even Car Wash prosecutors acknowledged Cardozo did not interfere in investigations, which many in Rousseff's base wanted him to do.

On a personal level, Cardozo represented one of the few open disagreements between creator and creature. Despite Lula's disapproval, Rousseff trusted her minister to the core. It would be unthinkable that she would blame her close friend for the obligatory testimony her mentor was giving at Congonhas airport. But she had to be aware that what was happening in that room with Lula could deeply affect her future.

---

45. Federal police released the full transcript of police questioning that day.

She and Lula had a long history. They met in the 1970s, when he was a union leader who challenged Brazil's dictatorship. While Rousseff was also opposed to the dictatorship, after being released from jail in 1973 she aimed for a normal life. Her then husband, Carlos Araújo, a labor attorney who had also taken up arms against the dictatorship, would be the link between her and Lula.

At that time, it was easier to imagine the friendly and eloquent Araújo, who would become a state legislator, one day running for president than to foresee his uncharismatic, down-to-earth and rigid wife as a politician. However, when the left won elections in the southern state of Rio Grande do Sul, or its capital Porto Alegre, in the 1980s and 1990s, it was the serious and organized Rousseff who was tapped for key roles: finance secretary in Porto Alegre and later the state's energy secretary.

Lula got to know her on visits to the region during presidential campaigns in 1989, 1994, 1998 and 2002. He would meet with her and Araújo, getting advice from the couple about connecting with voters in their state.

Rousseff's loyalty to Lula became evident in 2000, long before he ever decided to mentor her to be president. At the time, she was a member of the Democratic Labor Party, in large part thanks to the influence of Araújo and the charismatic leadership of Leonel Brizola, one of the biggest adversaries of the dictatorship.

Brizola, a former governor of both Rio Grande do Sul and Rio de Janeiro states, was a Lula rival on the left. Brizola used to say, and Rousseff sometimes openly agreed, that Lula had become too much of a conciliator, didn't have enough experience to govern and would struggle to get a base in the country's fractured Congress — if he ever got elected president.

But as the center-right presidency of Fernando Henrique Cardoso struggled two years before the 2002 elections, it was the former union leader, not Brizola, who appeared to be on a path to victory.

In 2000, Rousseff, then energy secretary in Rio Grande do Sul, left Brizola's party for the Workers' Party. The switch quickly bore fruit. Rousseff was invited to work on the Workers' Party energy program. As a budget specialist, she learned that then-President Cardoso was preparing to invest billions of dollars in Petrobras to build oil rigs. However, none of them were going to be built in Brazil.

Rousseff showed her findings to Gleisi Hoffmann, at the time a close friend of Lula. Spin-doctor Duda Mendonça celebrated that information with a party. That discovery became one of the centerpieces of Lula's platform: He scored points with ads insisting he wanted jobs for Brazilians, while the current government was shipping them overseas.

Rousseff was quickly included in Lula's government transition team. After a couple of weeks, the president-elect decided to give the energy minister post to "that gaucha Dilma who is always carrying a laptop and looking grumpy," Araújo recalled Lula telling him. He added that Rousseff's frankness got Lula's attention from the first Cabinet meeting.[46]

During the entire meeting, Rousseff did not utter a word. She only shook her head when then Central Bank governor Henrique Meirelles began to speak about Brazil's budget for that year.

After the meeting ended, Lula asked Rousseff what was wrong.

"Meirelles is hiding the milk, Mr. President," Araújo recounted Rousseff replying.

The implication was that Meirelles should not be trusted due to his close links to Wall Street and major Brazilian banks. A friendship between Rousseff and Lula emerged from private classes the minister

---

46. How Rousseff impressed Lula in their early years working together is documented at length in "Vultos da República," a compilation of profiles done by magazine *Piauí*.

gave the president on how to read budgets so he would never "be fooled" in the future.[47]

Lula kept his admiration for Meirelles, as he liked to have different, often adversarial opinions in his administration. But after that, Rousseff entered his circle of trust.

"Dilminha," as he called her, would be 100 percent frank, unlike other ministers who dreamed of running for president, such as Chief of Staff José Dirceu, Finance Minister Antonio Palocci or Science and Technology Minister Eduardo Campos, a man Lula considered to be like a son.

The frankness worked the other way when Rousseff became president, with Lula often saying what he thought his protégée should be doing. Such unsolicited advice even came out the day Lula was being interrogated.

"If I was Dilma, I would be traveling abroad each month to sell things from Brazil," Lula told investigators during one of his many tangents. "Why is she not traveling?"

As close as they were, Rousseff appeared to distance herself from Lula that Friday. In a statement, Rousseff wrote that the Car Wash "investigations must progress, so in the end there is punishment for whoever should be punished." However, she said that individual rights must be respected and that rushing to judgment "increased animosity and anti-democratic rhetoric" but did nothing to help find the truth.

"For that reason, I manifest my complete disagreement with the fact that a former president of the Republic who, on various occasions has voluntarily provided clarification to authorities, is now submitted to an

---

47. The account of Rousseff teaching Lula to better understand budgets came from ex-husband Araújo, quoted in magazine *Revista do Brasil*, in a piece published July 15, 2011.

unnecessary judicial summons to give testimony," she wrote.[48]

Rousseff was defending Lula's rights but not saying she believed he was innocent.

While Lula was being questioned, police searched his home, the Lula Institute and properties connected to his sons and other family members. One of his sons was also brought in for questioning. Meanwhile, small clashes broke out between supporters and detractors outside his home, adding to an environment of tension and uncertainty.

After about four hours, Lula was released. One of the most capable politicians of his generation then began a handful of speeches that felt more like campaign rallies than explanations aimed at defending his innocence.

"I felt like a prisoner this morning," said Lula, floating a run for president in 2018. "If they are a cent more honest than I am, then I will leave politics."[49]

On the same day that Car Wash got closer to him and political demise looked more likely for Rousseff in Brasília, Lula was already planning the next move. His mandatory testimony was the initial act of his attempt to return to the presidency. When many saw a former president nearing jail, Lula saw a lifeline to survive in case his protégée did not.

---

48. News portal *G1* quoted Rousseff on March 4, 2016.

49. Lula was quoted in daily *Estadão* on March 4, 2016.

From Rousseff's Early Days in Politics to Reelection in 2014

President Luiz Inácio Lula da Silva, on the right, speaks with Chief of Staff Dilma Rousseff during a meeting at the presidential palace in Brasília on Nov. 17, 2005. Rousseff gained Lula's trust by speaking her mind and was a close confident of the president during both of his administrations. (AP Photo/Eraldo Peres)

President Luiz Inácio Lula da Silva and Chief of Staff Dilma Rousseff are seen together at a ceremony for a sustainable program in the Amazon in this photo at the presidential palace in Brasília on May 8, 2008. (AP Photo/Eraldo Peres)

Sports Minister Orlando Silva speaks with Chief of Staff Dilma Rousseff during a press conference in Rio de Janeiro on April 30, 2009. The city would go on to win the bid to host the 2016 Summer Olympics, which added to the Lula administration's popularity. (AP Photo/Ricardo Moraes)

U.S. Secretary of State Hillary Rodham Clinton meets with President Luiz Inácio Lula da Silva and Chief of Staff Dilma Rousseff in Brasília on March 3, 2010. The Lula administration was popular with world leaders, particularly as millions moved out of poverty thanks to a commodities boom and social welfare programs. (AP Photo/Eraldo Peres)

President Luiz Inácio Lula da Silva raises the hand of Chief of Staff Dilma Rousseff during a Workers' Party meeting on Feb. 20, 2010. Lula and the party had named Rousseff as candidate for the presidential elections to take place later that year. (AP Photo/Eraldo Peres)

On her first day in office, Jan. 1, 2011, President Dilma Rousseff raises the hand of Vice President Michel Temer, seen on the left, and outgoing President Luiz Inácio Lula da Silva. To win the presidency, the Workers' Party had joined forces with Temer's centrist Brazilian Democratic Movement Party. (AP Photo/Silvia Izquierdo)

President Dilma Rousseff waves to supporters alongside her daughter, Paula, after being sworn in on Jan. 1, 2011. Before Rousseff, all Brazilian presidents had been men, and the customary thing on the first day in office was to greet supporters with their wives. Rousseff was divorced when she won the presidency. (AP Photo/Silvia Izquierdo)

President Dilma Rousseff meets with U.S. President Barack Obama and his family in Brasília on March 19, 2011. On the coattails of her predecessor, Rousseff was initially popular in the country and was a draw for foreign leaders. (AP Photo/Susan Walsh)

Thousands demonstrate against public transportation fare hikes and the Rousseff administration in Rio de Janeiro on June 24, 2013. What began as angst over fare hikes in São Paulo morphed into widespread protests that were the first signs of growing discontent with the Rousseff administration. (AP Photo/Felipe Dana)

President Dilma Rousseff speaks at the Workers' Party national convention in Brasília on June 21, 2014. While her popularity had fallen compared to the beginning of her presidency, the party supported Rousseff's reelection bid on the ticket along with Vice President Michel Temer. (AP Photo/Eraldo Peres)

Venezuelan President Nicolas Maduro presents a photograph to late President Hugo Chavez on May 9, 2013. While most Rousseff policies were moderate compared to leaders like Maduro, the president and her Workers' Party were decidedly leftist in their ideology and relationships with many foreign leaders. (AP Photo/Eraldo Peres)

In this photo taken on July 28, 2013, from left President Dilma Rousseff is seen meeting Uruguayan Vice President Danilo Astori, Pope Francis, Bolivian President Evo Morales and Argentine President Cristina Fernandez. (AP Photo/Brazil's Presidential Press Office/ Roberto Stuckert Filho)

In full reelection campaign mode, President Dilma Rousseff meets supporters during a gathering of artists in Rio de Janeiro on Sept. 15, 2014. (AP Photo/Silvia Izquierdo)

Aécio Neves, candidate of the Brazilian Social Democracy Party, greets supporters in Rio Janeiro on Oct. 19, 2014. Rousseff and Neves would face off during the presidential runoff, with Rousseff winning by just a few percentage points. (AP Photo/Felipe Dana)

President Dilma Rousseff makes the symbol of a heart while greeting supporters on Oct. 20, 2014 in Rio de Janeiro. Just days later, she would win reelection by a tight margin. (AP Photo/Silvia Izquierdo)

President Dilma Rousseff meets with U.S. Vice President Joe Biden on the first day in office of her second term, Jan. 1, 2015. In the background Vice President Michel Temer is seen looking on. In breaking with Rousseff ahead of impeachment in late 2015, in a leaked letter Temer expressed frustration that he was not invited to a private meeting with Biden that day. (AP Photo/Eraldo Peres)

CHAPTER 9

Crackdown on Elite

It was no surprise that Marcelo Odebrecht, CEO of the massive construction firm Odebrecht and heir to its founders, was convicted by Judge Sergio Moro. Odebrecht had been in jail since being arrested in June 2015 on charges of corruption, money laundering and belonging to a criminal organization.

But the length of the sentence handed down on March 6, 2016 — 19 years and four months — given to one of Brazil's most powerful and wealthy men, underscored the growing force of the Car Wash investigation. Since the first arrests in March 2014, the probe into kickbacks to politicians and other officials via inflated construction contracts was challenging Brazil's elite and ruling class in unprecedented ways.

Historically in Brazil, one of the world's most unequal countries, people like Odebrecht rarely did real jail time. If they were arrested for committing a crime and convicted, both rare occurrences, they were given a slap on the wrist at most.

Throughout much of the 20th century, Brazilians grew up hearing that construction companies were the "owners" of Brazil. And who could argue otherwise? Any bad acting aside, these firms were building highways in the jungle, hydroelectric dams that would bring power to millions of Brazilian households and metro systems in the largest cities. The Workers' Party governments, far from trying to check the power of these companies, embraced them.

Lula and Rousseff even had a policy of "national champions" that aimed at helping these firms become global players, yet one more way that a rising Brazil would make its mark on the world stage. What it meant was access to cheap state loans and the support of the government.

While on the surface Odebrecht's conviction wasn't related to Rousseff, indirectly it damaged her in several ways. That a person of Odebrecht's stature could be toppled meant that nobody, even a president, was safe from the swelling forces in the country that reflected a growing feeling that enough was enough of the corruption. It was also a strong blow to the government-business partnership that flourished under the Workers' Party and brought corruption and campaign finance into view.

Not long before he was arrested, as the Car Wash investigation was gaining steam, Odebrecht had said during a seminar in São Paulo that he was "irritated that we are in the line of fire of political clashes. We are the ones who generate employment."[50]

Lula frequently made similar comments, even at rallies where he would defend Rousseff against the impeachment push.

"Now I want you all to seek out the (Car Wash) task force, seek out judge Moro to find out the following: If they are talking about how much this operation has hurt the Brazilian economy," Lula told union workers. "You have to seek out the task force and ask if they are conscious about what is happening in the country."[51]

Comments like these were indicative of the special status that businesses enjoyed. It was no surprise then that men like Odebrecht saw themselves as patriarchs doing what was best for the country. For Odebrecht, the close connection with the government began long before the Workers' Party took over the presidency in 2003.

Founded in 1944, the Odebrecht company built close relationships with politicians in the 1950s, when the board of state-run oil company Petrobras was composed of military personnel from Bahia state, where Odebrecht had its headquarters for decades.

During the 1964-1985 military rule, the company focused lobbying efforts on executives and government agencies, and much money was spent to gain government favor. Such investments in the coffers of politicians clearly produced worthwhile returns.

"For each dollar paid in bribes, they got $10 back in contracts," estimated historian and Odebrecht scholar Pedro Henrique Campos.[52]

By the 1970s, the company had landed its first large-scale contracts

---

50. Recounted in article published by BBC Brasil on Aug. 3, 2016.
51. Footage of Lula speaking was broadcast by news program Jornal Nacional on March 24, 2016.
52. Interviewed by AP's Peter Prengaman and Mauricio Savarese.

outside of Bahia, including the building of a nuclear plant and the Galeão International Airport in Rio de Janeiro. In that decade, it also began an expansion to a handful of countries in Latin America and Africa, decades later making it one of the world's largest construction conglomerates.

"A small, local company grew in the shadows" of Brazil's construction boom, said Campos.

As Brazil changed, Odebrecht evolved. When democracy returned in the 1980s, Odebrecht added political parties to its payroll, along with many individual lawmakers and even willing journalists. Scandals began to emerge, as the military's fall meant that keeping corruption under wraps was impossible. Still, none of it appeared to present a big problem for Odebrecht.

In 1992, police interrogated then CEO Emilio Odebrecht, the father of Marcelo, about alleged bribes of $3.2 million paid to the campaign treasurer of then President Fernando Collor de Mello. At the time, the company said the payments were for consulting work.

In 1993, Odebrecht was linked to corruption after dozens of floppy discs were seized at the home of top company executive Manoel Ailton Soares dos Reis. More than 350 politicians were named in one of the documents recovered. Dos Reis, who never faced charges, told a congressional commission that the hundreds of names on the discs amounted to "personal and subjective evaluations to establish internal criteria for eventual and future campaign collaborations."[53]

"It all ended in pizza," as Brazilians say when investigations don't bear fruit.

Shortly before the 1994 presidential election, Emilio Odebrecht, in a blunt and nonchalant way, even acknowledged paying bribes.

"I am not going to say that we are an innocent company," he told the

---

53. Dos Reis' 1993 testimony was recounted in a Dec. 18, 2016, article by daily *Folha de S.Paulo.*

newspaper *Folha de S.Paulo*. "To survive in this field, I did (pay bribes). But if you ask me when and to whom, I will never tell you."[54]

A leading lawmaker who pushed to prosecute Odebrecht in the floppy disc case, former Sen. José Paulo Bisol, said his career was subsequently derailed.

"Odebrecht was the owner of Brazil and no one wanted to step on its foot," said Bisol.[55] "Those who did paid the price, and I was one of them."

Bisol had been a respected socialist lawmaker and legal expert. Then presidential candidate Lula picked him as his vice-presidential running mate in 1994. But Bisol was forced out amid corruption allegations that were never proven.

"Isn't it a huge coincidence that after decades of a clean political life and after being a judge for so long, this suddenly appears right after I went after them?" said Bisol.

For decades, Odebrecht weathered many scandals and always emerged on top. The Car Wash probe would change that.

For the first year of the probe, Odebrecht was able to deflect blame to Petrobras, where the investigation had begun. But arrests of business executives, including at Odebrecht, got higher and higher up the chain. By the time Marcelo Odebrecht was convicted, several other big fish in the construction world had already been brought down. The growing list included top executives of Mendes Junior, OAS, Galvão Engenharia, Engevix, Camargo Corrêa and Carioca Engenharia.

The central thrust of Marcelo Odebrecht's defense had been that as CEO he was too high up in the organization to know what underlings in Odebrecht or even top officials in the overall conglomerate, which included

---

54. Emilio Odebrecht was quoted in a *Folha de S.Paulo* article published June 26, 1994.

55. Bisol was interviewed by AP's Mauricio Savarese. Bisol died in June 2021 at age 92.

several companies, were doing. However, Moro cited emails recovered by investigators showing Odebrecht did in fact know what was going on. The judge concluded the CEO had actually been directing traffic.

"These multimillion-dollar operations were structured and refined and only could have been done in an organized way by people in control of the holding company and its main companies," wrote Moro in the sentence.[56]

Moro cited a message in which Rogério Araújo, an Odebrecht executive, copied Marcelo Odebrecht. In it, Araújo said he had access to a list of companies that Petrobras planned to invite for a tender.

"So the contention that Marcelo Bahia Odebrecht kept himself, in Olympic fashion, away from the business of each unit (of the holding company) and they operated in complete autonomy is not consistent with the documentary evidence of the case," Moro wrote.[57]

The conviction made good on the promise implicit in the name of the police operation that netted Odebrecht and several other executives the year before: "Erga omnes," Latin meaning "valid for all."

Rousseff had no connection to that operation nor what led to Odebrecht's conviction. However, members of her party were engulfed in the Car Wash investigation; the case against Odebrecht was one more galling example of just how far the corruption went.

And with the Chamber of Deputies on the cusp of taking up impeachment legislation, the downfall of one of Brazil's most powerful companies, a construction giant that had played such a key role the nation's modern history, added to a growing feeling among average Brazilians that the country had lost its way and the only solution was a major shakeup of the political class.

---

56. Marcelo Odebrecht's sentence was published in *Jornal Jurid* on March 8, 2016.

57. Sections of Moro's ruling were published in news website *Jornal de Brasília* on March 8, 2016.

CHAPTER 10

The Street Erupts

It would be a national protest that one newspaper would call "the biggest in history."

Organized to demand Rousseff's impeachment, Brazilians also took to the streets angry about corruption and the sprawling Car Wash investigation. Some focused their ire on Lula, who had just recently been forced by authorities to answer questions about one of many corruption cases being built against him. Protesters got plenty of nudging to get out: Soccer games were postponed; hours were extended on the subway system in São Paulo, the nation's biggest city; and wall-to-wall media coverage filled the days leading up to it.

To reach that level of organization is rare in a country where military and police brutality have historically discouraged people from protesting. While allowed since the return to democracy, demonstrations were often broken up, particularly when organized by left-leaning groups targeting the government, the wealthy or major industries.

The March 13, 2016, protest would be different from other protests for many reasons. Relatively new groups, some on the margins and all with a strong online presence, would lead the organizational charge by employing a mix of social media encouraging people to come out and false news stories about left-leaning leaders. Stories on alleged voter fraud or Workers' Party politicians supposedly cashing in on bribes, sometimes with heavily doctored videos, oozed through the messaging service WhatsApp.

Most politicians, no matter how conservative, were not welcomed. Defeated 2014 presidential candidate Aécio Neves was even jeered in São Paulo. That didn't stop him, however, from calling for Rousseff to be removed by impeachment, by annulling her 2014 campaign or by her resignation.

"Any way that gets the current president out of office, respecting our constitution, would be better than extending this death walk for the Brazilian people more years," Neves said during an appearance on the same day in his home city of Belo Horizonte.[58]

Extremists on the right sided with Congressman Jair Bolsonaro, who pledged to govern with a full military cabinet if he became president. Some wanted to take it even a step further: a military coup.

Some of the anti-Rousseff chants and signs were laden with sexist attacks. "With that balance, the ho falls," read a big sign in the

---

58. Neves was quoted by news website *R7* on March 13, 2016.

northeastern city of Recife. Focusing on Rousseff's gender, often in vulgar ways, had been a constant in protests against her government.

The only person to get nearly unanimous praise on the streets on March 13 was Sergio Moro, the federal judge leading the mushrooming Car Wash investigation. Livid over the cases of alleged jaw-dropping graft coming out daily in the news and anxious about the tumbling economy, many Brazilians felt Moro represented a lone bright spot amid an otherwise bleak horizon. Some protesters chanted Moro's name, pumped signs that said, "I Love Sergio Moro!," "We Are All Moro," and "In Moro We Trust." Others carried flags with his picture and papier-mâché statues of his likeness.

While Moro didn't participate in the demonstrations, the judge, known for his savvy use of the media, made sure his voice was heard. In a statement carried widely, Moro said that Brazilians had come out to protest corruption and that he "was touched" by the support for the Car Wash investigations. "There is no future with systematic corruption that destroys our democracy, our economic well-being and our dignity as a country." Moro didn't use the word "impeachment" or name anybody in the Workers' Party. He didn't need to. For many Brazilians, it would be natural to conclude that Moro supported Rousseff's ouster.[59]

Very few of the people going to the streets knew much about Vice President Michel Temer, the man who would take over if Rousseff was toppled. Many believed that as soon as she was removed, Temer and Cunha would follow, and Brazil would be cleaned of corruption and poor governance.

With Rousseff's administration in political and economic freefall, conservatives were excited on that historic Sunday. They had already successfully organized several large demonstrations since the president was re-elected, though none this size.

---

59. News portal *G1* did an entire piece around Moro's statement on March 13, 2016.

Meanwhile, progressives, who used to own the streets for their causes and sometimes clashed with police, knew they now could not outnumber adversaries who were usually more pacifist.

Brazil's mainstream media companies did their part; after publicizing the event days in advance they provided live coverage as it unfolded. That Sunday morning, in talking about rescheduled soccer games, sports programs and cable TV news made sure to tell their viewers that nation-wide protests were planned.

In the heartland of the movement, São Paulo Gov. Geraldo Alckmin had given his own push by authorizing an hour of overtime for subway workers that day, thus ensuring more trains. It was a striking move, as his administration had been cutting service amid budget deficits. Still, it wasn't the first time Alckmin, a member of Neves' party with his own presidential ambitions, had extended such a hand. During a large anti-Rousseff protest the previous year, subway authorities temporarily didn't charge riders going to Paulista Avenue, where the demonstration was centered.[60]

"The country can't lose time," Alckmin said during a press conference the morning of March 13. "It's necessary to move toward a fast solution so as to return to growth, employment and quality of life for our people."

Protesters started showing up early, many donning Brazil's national soccer team shirts and carrying banners calling for the end of the Workers' Party and for Rousseff's impeachment. In many parts of the country, local media showed anti-left demonstrators hugging policemen as if they were part of the movement.

A Datafolha institute poll taken that Sunday and published the following day, found that most protesters were highly educated, upper-middle-class white men in their mid-30s. Put another way, for many going to

---

60. An article in news website *Valor* on March 18, 2015, explains the temporary lifting of ticket gates during an anti-Rousseff protest.

Paulista Avenue, all they had to do was take the elevators in their buildings and go out on the street.

Perhaps most tellingly, when asked to name the best president in Brazil's history, 60 percent of respondents said Fernando Henrique Cardoso, a highly successful sociologist-turned-president who was in office between 1995 and 2002. On the other hand, Cardoso's successor, Lula, who would leave office at the end of 2010 with the highest approval ratings of any Brazilian president in modern history, was the top choice for only 2 percent of respondents.[61]

Remarkably, just a month before, a similar question on a nationwide poll found that just 15 percent believed Cardoso was the best president in the nation's history. By comparison, 37 percent believed it was Lula.[62]

"We are here because we are not stupid like those people the government buys with social programs," engineer Claudio Alves, 42, argued as he walked with his family on Paulista Avenue. "We are well informed."

Adversaries gave people like Alves the nickname "coxinha," the name of a popular Brazilian chicken croquette. In response, pro-impeachment demonstrators called their antagonists "mortadela," a reference to cheap baloney sandwiches that leftist movement organizers have historically offered supporters at protests.

"I came here for free," Alves yelled as he marched.[63]

The atmosphere, though, was not one of outrage. The gatherings were carnivalesque, with beer and whiskey flowing from the beginning at about 10 a.m. and continuing well into the evening. Flirtatious young men and women sat on the sidewalks wearing yellow and green, the colors of Brazil's flag, some using "Fora PT," or "Down with the Workers' Party," as an opening line. Music boomed from loudspeakers, which got

---

61. Datafolha poll published March 14, 2016.
62. Datafolha poll published Feb. 29, 2016.
63. AP's Mauricio Savarese interviewed Alves and covered the protest that day.

much more attention than the words of leaders of the citizen groups Movimento Brasil Livre, or Free Brazil Movement, and Vem pra Rua, or Come to the Street. When far-right protesters wishing for a military coup or monarchists spoke, most protesters laughed or looked away.

Reporters for major news organizations, chiefly TV Globo, experienced something unheard of at protests organized by left-leaning groups: They were greeted warmly by many in the streets, one exception being far right supporters, many wearing banners with the name of lawmaker Jair Bolsonaro. Police were busy, but not because they were called to action; officers took selfies with some impeachment advocates.

The president's base considered going to Paulista Avenue as well, but the unions that would have bused people in decided to skip it, so as to avoid any clashes. They scheduled their own demonstration for March 18, the following Friday.

Throughout the day, younger left-leaning Brazilians criticized conservatives online, but their voices were drowned out. On television, the massive protest underscored Rousseff's perilous situation, making her look weak and with little support.

Protesters in São Paulo blocked traffic on several streets. A giant yellow plastic duck also got attention in the crowds and was the focus of many news photographs and video pieces that day. The duck had been provided by the country's top industry group, the Industrial Federation of São Paulo state, known as FIESP. Meant to be a symbol against increased taxes, the implication was that average Brazilians should not have to pay the costs of poor governance and needless spending, allegedly being done by the Rousseff administration. As part of the anti-tax campaign, giant ducks had been used in previous protests and even placed on the esplanade in Brasília.

Whether or not those on the streets were aware, the leader of FIESP, textile businessman Paulo Skaf, was also a close friend of Temer.

Rousseff stayed in the presidential palace in Brasília all day, not making any public appearances. The night before, she called for the protests to be peaceful, also subtly telling Brazilians why she should not be impeached.

"I have lived at a time when if you protested, you were jailed. If you disagreed (with the government), you were jailed. For us, now that is not the case," Rousseff wrote. "We live in a time when people can protest, can express what they think, and that is something we must preserve."[64]

Late on that protest day, Rousseff put out a statement that again celebrated democracy. "The peaceful character of this Sunday's demonstrations shows the maturity of a country that knows how to co-exist with different opinions and knows how to secure respect for its laws and institutions," she wrote.[65]

While the March 13 protest was a major strike against Rousseff, its base had formed a few years before. Historians and political analysts point to Oct. 26, 2014, the day of the second round of the election, as a key moment in Brazil's polarization.

When Rousseff was announced winner by a small margin in her quest for reelection, millions of angry Brazilians who did not vote for her challenged the results. Not that there were objective reasons to believe there had been fraud: By all accounts, voting had been clean.

For many conservative political pundits helping to foment anger at Rousseff, however, the actual election results seemed secondary. Consider an exchange on the night of the election at a moment when 95 percent of returns were in and less than 1 percent separated the two candidates.

Joice Hasselmann, hostess of TV *Veja*, an online channel that belonged to the magazine, said Rousseff would have trouble staying on the job even if reelected.

"There is the issue of black money deal maker Alberto Yousseff," said

---

64. Published in daily *Estadão* on March 13, 2016.
65. Quoted in The Associated Press story from March 13, 2016.

Hasselmann, referring to the man whose testimony helped turn Car Wash into a mega scandal by implicating numerous politicians and business leaders. "Everything suggests (his accusations) will be proved, he did a plea bargain deal and needs to introduce evidence, otherwise the judge will not accept it . . . we have a likely impeachment process ahead."

Veteran journalist Ricardo Setti, appearing on the show, agreed. "We have the possibility of impeachment," he said, adding that in that case, "Michel Temer will be president. The PMDB will be in power."

Many Brazilians thought removing presidents could only bring better days, as when President Fernando Collor de Mello was shown out for blatant corruption involving himself and his entourage. Comparing Collor, who had been a friend of Brazilian dictators, to left-leaning presidents Rousseff and Lula was a common insult levied by conservatives. It also helped justify what they believed should come next: ousting Rousseff.

More moderate opposition leaders noted how small Rousseff's mandate was after such a tight victory over Neves. Making matters worse for the left, Rousseff would have to deal with the most conservative Congress in decades. Being president was not going to equal an ability to really govern, or at the very least accomplish much legislatively.

Opposition leaders, bitter about her win, openly talked about blocking any meaningful initiatives in Congress as a way of stopping Lula from returning to the fold and winning the 2018 presidential elections.

Moderate critics who did not believe in impeachment as a solution, at least at first, noticed that even heavyweight politicians of the Workers' Party stayed away from the former urban guerrilla when she formed her Cabinet.

Lula, who had a scant presence in critical stages of the race, had done little to ease the tensions within his party or with the social movements that respected his leadership. For her part, Rousseff had not accepted Lula's suggestion to appoint former central bank governor Henrique Meirelles as finance minister. Instead, she went with bureaucrat

Joaquim Levy, a conservative who angered moderates.

For detractors of Rousseff and the Workers' Party, there was a dilemma: If they couldn't beat Rousseff at her worst moment despite a number of corruption scandals in her party and in her administration, and when the economy was no longer booming, when would they be able to win? For many on the right, the math was terrifying. Lula had been president between 2003 and 2010. Rousseff was elected to be president between 2011 and 2018. If Lula then returned and was re-elected, he could be president from 2019 through 2026.

But it wasn't just people on the right who were angry. There was plenty of frustration across the spectrum, especially in a middle class that did not see their lot improve as much as the poor did and yearned for less government spending and more efficient services. Many of those people argued that the Workers' Party had bought off marginalized Brazilians and locked the country into heavy spending by raising the minimum wage and instituting social welfare programs like Bolsa Familia, or Family Stipend, which gives small monthly checks to the extreme poor, and Minha Casa, Minha Vida, or My House, My Life, which provides subsidies for low-income families to own homes.

Some critics also believed the left-leaning party was actually radical and wanted to capture the Brazilian state Soviet-style, worries not based on facts. A few ill-informed voters were angered over fake news stories. Among the faux tales that spread virally on WhatsApp:

— Ballots had been tampered with in several areas.
— The Workers' Party paid hefty sums to people in impoverished areas to support Rousseff.
— Enemies of the left were poisoned in prison after signing plea bargains.
— Doctored pictures appeared of a young Rousseff shooting a gun on the street during her time fighting against the dictatorship.

The atmosphere was so toxic in the days after Rousseff's victory that hardcore critics spent days walking around Brazilian cities with the cover of conservative magazine *Veja* tied to their necks. The publication, known both for scoops and frivolous tabloid stories, had of course suggested Rousseff and Lula knew that high-ranking officials of state-run oil giant Petrobras were being paid bribes to illegally fund their presidential bids. Brazil's electoral court, despite being headed by a judge who did not sympathize with the president, stopped *Veja* from using that cover on billboards and labelled it as propaganda. *Veja* protested, but the decision stood.

By the time the March 13 protests happened, about a year and a half after Rousseff's close victory, there were many backstories and a lot of political baggage across Brazilian society. Those things could never, however, be captured in an image of mass protest or a newspaper headline.

The day after the march, the conservative daily *O Globo*'s headline read, "Brazil takes to the streets against Lula and Dilma and for Moro." The cover of daily *Estado de S.Paulo*, also conservative, had nothing but a picture of the protest on Paulista Avenue and the date. *Folha de S.Paulo*, arguably the most balanced of the three big dailies, said, "Anti-Dilma protest is the biggest in history."

Folha de S.Paulo counted 500,000 people on Paulista Avenue, 100,000 more than a major pro-democracy protest in 1984. Only a Mass led by Pope Francis in Rio de Janeiro in 2013 drew more people, around 865,000, according to the newspaper's pollster Datafolha.

The protests were not limited to São Paulo. There were demonstrations in more than 400 cities. In Rio de Janeiro, a protest spread out for several blocks along Copacabana Beach. In Brasília, thousands paraded near the presidential palace, Congress and Supreme Federal Tribunal. In the northeast, a stronghold for Rousseff and Lula, there were also several protests, though in much smaller numbers. News organizations tallied police counts in the various cities and came to more than 3.6 million people protesting nationwide.[66] Organizers said they estimated nearly 7 million.

Most reports made reference to orderly Brazilians of all kinds taking to the streets nationwide against Rousseff, Lula, corruption and poor governance. Polls later that week suggested the poor were also upset with corruption and Rousseff's tumbling government, but most of them did not feel they should be part of the yellow-and-green protests.

Ironically, the overall anti-Workers' Party narrative suited politicians from other parties who were also targeted by protesters, including many in Temer's party accused of corruption. Their own shortcomings aside, they didn't hesitate to pin the nation's problems on the Workers' Party and its embattled leaders.

Workers' Party officials had their own narrative that minimized the focus on Rousseff. "I am worried because in 1964 the coup mongers supported the military and there were 21 years of a bloody dictatorship," said Rui Falcão, president of the Workers' Party.[67]

With the streets clearly lost to her adversaries, Rousseff appeared to start moving toward giving the presidency away. Not by resigning. She would never make that decision.

66. News portal *G1* did this tally the day after the protest, on March 14, 2016.
67. Quoted in *Folha de S.Paulo* on March 17, 2016.

CHAPTER 11

'Leaks Serve a Useful Purpose'

Sergio Fernando Moro was born in 1972, at the peak of Brazil's military dictatorship, in the southern state of Paraná. His parents, both schoolteachers, fostered in him a love of learning that led to his earning undergraduate and master's degrees and a doctorate, all in law from universities in his home state. He also participated in an exchange program for lawyers at Harvard University.[68]

At 24 years old, Moro scored high enough on a national exam to become a judge in Curitiba, the capital of Paraná. While Moro got his career off to a strong start, Curitiba was a second-tier destination in legal circles, as the most important courts and law firms were in cities like São Paulo, Rio de Janeiro, Brasília, Belo Horizonte and Porto Alegre.

In his first years, Moro ruled on cases ranging from pensions to money laundering. He gained a reputation for writing meticulous decisions faster than many Brazilian judges and rarely had his rulings overturned by higher courts. By 2012, Moro was seen as such an expert in money laundering cases that Rosa Maria Weber, a justice on the Supreme Federal Tribunal, asked him to assist in the Mensalão investigation and trial into alleged vote buying.

The scheme, which came to light in 2005, involved alleged payments to many members of the Chamber of Deputies, via money funneled through state-owned companies, for their votes in favor of legislation supported by the administration of then President Luiz Inácio Lula da Silva. The scandal implicated several parties and threatened Lula's government.

Moro clearly brought the seasoning he gained from the Mensalão probe and other experiences to the Car Wash investigation when it began in early 2014.

Vladimir Netto, a journalist for GloboNews who wrote *Car Wash: Judge Sergio Moro and Behind the Scenes of the Operation That Rocked Brazil*, said Moro had become a formidable obstacle for many of the country's best lawyers.

---

68. Moro's life and trajectory are well documented. An article published in April 2016 by news website *GZH Geral* lists his educational history and some accolades.

"These guys are used to always winning, but they have not this time," said Netto.[69]

A decade before Moro became famous, he wrote a paper for a legal journal on the Italian authorities who took on the Mafia in the 1990s.[70] That colossal corruption probe, "Operation Clean Hands," would bring down many of Italy's elite and rejigger the political order.

In the 2004 article, Moro reviewed the investigation in a way that many would later interpret as a blueprint for what he hoped to achieve at home. He noted how Italian judges used plea bargains to advance investigations, kept suspects in jail while their cases were processed and took advantage of news media to shape public opinion.

"Leaks serve a useful purpose," Moro wrote. "The constant flow of revelations keeps public interest up and party leaders on the defensive."

More than just facilitating leaks, Moro argued that judges need to get a corruption-fatigued public on their side to give weight to investigations. In sum, the more the political establishment was on the ropes, the more power the judicial system would wield. Moro put all of that to work from the beginning of the wide-ranging probe in Brazil.

"The Car Wash investigation could not have just one hero. There are judges, prosecutors, detectives," said Igor Romário, the lead federal police investigator on the case.[71] "But Moro is the center of it. Without him, we wouldn't be where we are."

That Romario, or any Brazilian for that matter, spoke about a judge as a "hero" underscored Moro's uniqueness—or partisanship, as detractors argued. After all, investigators work to uncover wrongdoing, prosecutors then try to prove it in court, and then it's up to a judge or a jury, or both, to decide on the merits of the case.

---

69. AP's Peter Prengaman interviewed Netto in January 2017.
70. Moro's full article was published by legal website Consultor Jurídico in 2004.
71. AP's Peter Prengaman interviewed Romário in January 2017

One of Moro's initial decisions in 2014, which helped turn Car Wash into a mega case, was to accept a plea bargain from black-money dealer Alberto Yousseff. It wasn't Moro's first time dealing with Yousseff.

In 2004, Yousseff had reached a plea bargain over a massive fraud case in Paraná. His testimony — he admitted moving millions of dollars illegally — helped the judge arrest other dirty money dealers in the region. With many competitors in jail, Yousseff went back to his old ways. That helped him channel bribes for much bigger fish, such as Petrobras executives and top politicians.

In building the investigation into the largest corruption probe in Brazilian history, Moro had to overcome numerous obstacles. He could have been blocked from taking the operation further since Petrobras' headquarters were in Rio de Janeiro, not in his jurisdiction in distant Paraná. Jurisdictional challenges could have thwarted him at many points, since many of the alleged crimes took place at political offices in Brasília. Indeed, defense attorneys, along with legal experts, frequently argued that many of the major Car Wash cases should never have even been before Moro. By combining shrewd structuring of the cases, a strong relationship with the press and growing public adoration, Moro always found a way to keep control of the investigation.

A desire to maintain control and not let one of the biggest fish being targeted escape his jurisdiction clearly influenced Moro to make arguably the boldest, and riskiest, decision of his career: to release wiretapped conversations between Rousseff and Lula that raised suspicion of obstruction of justice.

Those conversations, which dominated headlines and water cooler chats for days, had the effect of a grenade rolled across Brazil's political landscape — albeit with a sharp debate about whether there was ever enough powder for an explosion.

For weeks, there had been reports that Lula would join Rousseff's government as chief of staff. Such a move would be significant in several ways.

In bringing Lula on, Rousseff would be effectively acknowledging that her presidency was over. Sure, she would remain the figurehead, but few could imagine that her predecessor, her creator and potential successor, would be doing anything less than calling the shots. It would also be an acknowledgement that despite outward optimism, the Workers' Party and Rousseff recognized she was vulnerable in the upcoming impeachment process.

Lula, a consummate people person who had successfully led Brazil for eight years, could certainly help Rousseff change the equation in Brasília. Upon confirming the rumors, Rousseff even said as much.

"Let's be honest," Rousseff told reporters in Brasília on March 16, 2016, the day before Lula was to be confirmed. "Lula will strengthen my government. There are people who don't want it strengthened."[72]

At the same time, many adversaries of the president, including Cunha, worried that the impeachment process would be derailed if Lula became chief of staff.[73]

In that same press conference, Rousseff commended Lula's "unquestionable political experience," deft handling of the economy as president and "knowledge of the country and commitment to political and strategic visions."

But Lula also had mounting legal baggage, which presented risks for Rousseff. Less than two weeks before, he had been obligated to submit testimony about a handful of corruption cases being built against him. The slow wheels of the justice system meant that a conviction was not imminent, and jail time for any conviction would be even further off

---

72. Rousseff was quoted by daily *Exame* on March 16, 2016.

73. In his book published in 2021, Cunha said: "If Lula had become chief-of-staff at that time and put Temer as justice minister — which he might have accepted for Lula would become de facto president — I believe the moves for impeachment would die, Dilma would save herself and the economy would separate from the political crisis."

thanks to his ability to appeal. Still, Lula in her government wouldn't be a good look, and many important figures in Brazil were quick to criticize Rousseff.

"Politically speaking, I think society has to act strongly against this," said former President Fernando Henrique Cardoso.[74] "I think it's scandalous that a person can become a minister at the same moment when he could become a defendant (in a criminal case). It's very strange. It adds to the moral crisis."

In reality, such a situation wasn't unique. An estimated 60 percent of the members of the Chamber of Deputies gearing up to vote on impeachment legislation against Rousseff had either been charged with crimes or were being investigated, according to watchdog groups.[75] The congressman leading the charge against Rousseff, Eduardo Cunha, had so many legal woes that he could be arrested at any time.

It was amid this delicate situation that Moro released the wiretapped conversations between Rousseff and Lula. And the effect of doing so was immediate: That night, thousands took to the streets in several cities, with many calling for impeachment and others defending Rousseff. It was a decision that many deemed brave for putting the spotlight on a sitting president and others called illegal, partisan and ultimately damaging to Brazil's democracy.

For Moro, not interceding would also have consequences for Car Wash. If Lula became a member of the Cabinet, Moro would be required to send to the Supreme Federal Tribunal all documents obtained in the investigations into Lula. Brazil's top court would take over the investigation since only it can decide to prosecute, convict or jail federal lawmakers, including Cabinet members of a presidential administration. In practical terms,

---

74. Cardoso quoted by news portal G1 on March 16, 2016.
75. Fact-checking group Lupa published a list of members of Congress being investigated on April 17, 2016.

this privilege — "foro privilegiado" in the Brazilian legal term — that Lula would receive as a minister would get him out of Moro's jurisdiction.

In such a situation, the expectation would be that Moro would simply send the documents related to Lula investigations to the top court. Eventually the court, per its protocols, would release many of those documents to the public, though possibly years later. Moro clearly knew that releasing the documents even just a few months later would be too late; at that point, Lula would be ensconced in office.

For Moro, publishing the documents himself without delay would come with risks. One of the recordings included a conversation with Rousseff that could be interpreted as an attempt to obstruct justice. While that interpretation would be much debated, Rousseff clearly enjoyed the special protection of the highest court and the law of national security protected her phone calls. In other words, Moro would be stepping way out of bounds in releasing material that included a sitting president. The move could trigger an internal investigation against him.

Nonetheless, Moro decided to publish this and many other wiretaps related to Lula, even one of the former president's wife, Marisa Leticia, complaining about Rousseff detractors who banged pots at night to express their dissatisfaction. "Why don't they stick their pots in their asses," said the former first lady.

Also included in Moro's audio dump were phone conversations that Lula had with Rousseff's chief of staff, Jaques Wagner, Rio de Janeiro Mayor Eduardo Paes and Vagner Freitas, president of Unified Workers' Central, one of Brazil's main trade unions.

Thus, when the investigation was to be taken from his jurisdiction, the judge adopted the Italian prosecutors' strategy in "Operation Clean Hands": Bring in the press and hope that the public would side with the judge, even if he looked biased.

"Democracy in a free society requires that the governed know what their governors are doing, even when they seek to act within the protections of the shadows," Moro wrote in his decision.[76]

Many legal experts argued that both of Moro's decisions—to record the president and to release the conversations—were illegal, raising serious questions about the judge's objectivity. More importantly for an already polarized nation weeks away from the kickoff of impeachment proceedings, the recordings solidified and even hardened the positions of the pro- and anti-Rousseff camps.

Members of the Workers' Party in Congress and supporters characterized the recordings as inconsequential; they didn't prove a crime. Opposition parties and Workers' Party detractors had a different interpretation: that Rousseff and Lula were trying to obstruct justice by getting Lula out of Moro's jurisdiction and slowing the investigations against him.

The wiretap that got the most attention — an arguably inconclusive conversation between Rousseff and Lula about the formalities of being sworn in as her chief of staff — was reported by many news outlets as a blatant attempt to block the investigation.

Here is that short conversation in its entirety:

Dilma: "Hello."

Lula: "Hello."

Dilma: "Lula, let me tell you one thing."

Lula: "Go ahead, dear."

Dilma: "Next, I'm going to be sending Bessias to you with a paper so we have it, only to use it if necessary in the confirmation (of the Cabinet post)."

Lula: "That's fine. That's fine."

Dilma: "Just that. You wait there, as (Bessias) is on his way."

Lula: "That is fine. I'm here waiting."

Dilma: "Okay?"

76. Moro's decision published by news portal G1 on March 16, 2016.

Lula: "That's fine."

Dilma: "Bye."

Lula: "Bye, dear."

"Bessias" was Jorge Rodrigo Araújo Messias, a lawyer who was relatively unknown before becoming a protagonist mentioned and analyzed on every national television program. His name was mispronounced as "Bessias" by Rousseff because she had a cold at the time.

What exactly was he bringing to Lula? Why did this matter?

Rousseff's solicitor general, José Eduardo Cardozo, said the document was a "termo de posse," or instrument of investiture, which would allow Lula to take his position in the government by simply signing. Cardozo said it was only to be sent to Lula because his wife was feeling ill in São Paulo, and it wasn't clear if Lula would be able to make the ceremony in Brasília. (The former president's wife was known to suffer from a heart condition and died in 2017 after a stroke.)

Political adversaries did not believe the explanation. They thought the document was to be used in case a police raid was imminent. The country's most watched television news program, TV Globo's Jornal Nacional, apparently agreed.

"This Wednesday the political crisis that involves the Dilma Rousseff administration reached its highest point," said host William Bonner in a grave tone. "Before Lula took office as chief of staff, Judge Sergio Moro removed the secrecy of all the investigation on the former president. With that, phone conversations of the former president became public at the end of the afternoon. Members of the Car Wash task-force say there is evidence of activity to disrupt the investigations."

The three largest papers, *Folha de S.Paulo*, *O Globo* and *Estado de S.Paulo*, all interpreted the conversation in the same way. By then, all these news organizations had come out in favor of Rousseff's impeachment.

On social media, a famous Lula quote from the late 1980s, when he was a fiery union leader, reverberated: "In Brazil, when a poor person steals, he goes to jail. When a rich person does, he becomes a minister."

Other released recordings provided glimpses into the way that Lula and Workers' Party stalwarts viewed what was happening, both to him and to Rousseff.

In one conversation, Lula told Rousseff that the forced testimony that Moro had recently ordered had amounted to a "pyrotechnical spectacle," and he had little faith that he could get justice.

"I'm telling the Workers' Party here, Dilma, that there is no truce, there is no believing in the legal fight, we have to take our supporters and go to the streets," he said.

Lula said the Car Wash investigation had "intimidated" the Supreme Federal Tribunal and the Superior Court of Justice, the country's second highest court, along with members of government.

"We have a lower house speaker who is fucked, a president of the Senate who is fucked, I don't know how many parliament members threatened, everyone waiting for a miracle to happen, for everyone to be saved," he said, a statement that underscored the depths of the alleged corruption.

"I'm, honestly, scared of the Republic of Curitiba," said Lula sarcastically, adding that with Moro anything "can happen in this country."

Lula also told Rousseff that he "had wanted to retire" but the situation meant that he couldn't. Naturally, that meant he had to run for his old job.

"I'm moving up my campaign for 2018, I'm going to set up trips throughout this country starting next week, you know? I want to see what's going to happen. Unfortunately, it's going to be that, dear. I'm not sitting still at home."

In a conversation with Vagner Freitas, president of Unified Workers' Central, a major trade union founded by the Workers' Party in the 1980s, Lula recounted a conversation he apparently had had with Rousseff about fighting the impeachment momentum. He said Rousseff was trying to satisfy people who would oppose her no matter what.

"She is making policy for the sake of the market, which is her enemy.

No one from the market is going to vote for her," said Lula. "The market she is thinking of pleasing doesn't want pension reform... They want the end of pensions."

Moro later said he was sorry for the controversy caused by the publication of the audios, but he never said he regretted doing it.[77] The Supreme Federal Tribunal would later deem the recordings illegal, but there was no way to erase them from public consciousness. No action would be taken against Moro.

On the day the recordings came out, Lula told members of his party that there was only one solution: Put a more decisive presence of unionists and activists on the streets as a show of resistance. But could a former leader whose reputation had clearly been stained really inspire throngs to take the streets when many believed he and Rousseff were responsible for the corruption and economic decline?

Brazil was in chaos, and to many people, impeachment increasingly looked like a way to reestablish order.

---

77. Moro's apology to the court was published by news website G1 on March 29, 2016.

CHAPTER 12

Justice Intervenes

"Ladies and gentlemen," boomed the voice of the official announcer at Brazil's presidential palace as hundreds of members of the Workers' Party applauded and sang. "Here comes Madam President Dilma Rousseff, followed by former President Luiz Inácio Lula da Silva."

All television channels were broadcasting live as the two descended the spiral stairway toward the building's atrium. Rousseff, dressed in dark pants and white blazer, looked straight ahead and kept her usual stride while Lula, in a dark suit and red tie, waved to people in the audience:

Workers' Party leaders and lawmakers and Brasília insiders. When they reached the bottom, Rousseff went up on stage while Lula shook and slapped hands and hugged some in the first row. Smiley and chatty, Lula was returning to the presidential palace that he had left as a national hero on Jan. 1, 2011. Back then, he had an 87 percent approval rating.[78] Now, five years later, his support was much more modest. He and members of his family were under investigation. His protégée was at risk of being impeached. Many in the party he led, including some of his closest friends, were engulfed in the Car Wash investigation.

The palace event on March 17, 2016, putting a festive veneer on the gloom, was to formalize Lula's appointment as Rousseff's chief of staff. While the wiretap audios released by Judge Moro enraged many and hardened partisan positions, Lula and Rousseff behaved as if it was all business as usual.

After the short swearing-in ceremony, Rousseff spoke about the need for Brazil to get back to a "national project." Political fights and paralysis, she said, were "not in the interests of Brazilians."

But how many Brazilians were paying attention to Rousseff's words? Workers' Party insiders and detractors alike were pondering other questions. In becoming de facto president, could Lula save Rousseff from removal? And would his appointment to the Cabinet spare him from several corruption investigations, at least for a while?

A sign of how troubled Brazil would be after that ceremony came at the very end, when Congressman Major Olímpio, a populist former policeman allied with the far right and with Jair Bolsonaro, managed to get into the palace. "Shame! Shame!" he screamed as the former president signed documents to take office. As Olímpio was removed by security, adversaries of the embattled president were plotting their

---

78. News website *G1* cites polling group Ibope on Dec. 16, 2010.

next moves. Some would be made by a succession of judges.

Little-known federal judge Itagiba Catta Preta Neto was among the thousands who protested against Rousseff on Copacabana Beach in Rio de Janeiro hours after the audios were released. He proudly published pictures of himself at that protest on his social media channels wearing a yellow shirt, a common trend among pro-impeachment Brazilians.

The lower court judge, who almost immediately received an injunction request to block Lula's appointment to chief of staff, took little time in making his decision, as shown by online court records. In fact, just 28 seconds after a request was submitted by attorney Enio Meregalli Júnior, the judge granted it, according to the timestamps of the filings in courthouse records.[79] The decision came only about an hour after Lula took office in Brasília.

Neto's ruling had an immediate and powerful impact. Lula would appeal to the highest courts of the land, but until that was sorted out, he would be unable to help Rousseff. Meanwhile, Moro was once again in control.

The divide between Brazil's political leadership and the country's judiciary was more evident than ever. Not since the return of democracy in the late 1980s had a ministerial appointment been halted in this way. That made Palácio do Planalto insiders believe that the decision could soon be overruled. But the concerns were obvious.

Upon examination of Neto's social media activity, his political leanings were clear. On Facebook, he liked the pages of those opposed to the Workers' Party. He had already ruled against initiatives of the Rousseff administration, including one to bring Cuban doctors to Brazil to help

---

79. Daily *Jornal do Comércio*, recording the times of the Federal Justice website, reported on how quickly the judge entered the decision.

poor communities where few Brazilian medics were willing to work. Unions of Brazilian doctors argued the Cubans didn't have the necessary qualifications, and Neto sided with them from the start.

Neto had campaigned for Rousseff's adversary, Aécio Neves, in the 2014 presidential elections. And the night before his decision to block Lula, he posted on Facebook a picture of himself at a Rio de Janeiro protest, wearing futuristic glasses and smiling widely. His message was clear, even if not directly stated: "Fora, Dilma!" or "Out with Dilma!" the rallying cry of opponents.[80]

In his decision, the judge said it was apparent that the president was committing a crime in picking Lula. Between the lines, his ruling even suggested jail time for Rousseff.

Neto's reasoning was bold. He suggested Rousseff was not appointing Lula to save herself from impeachment, but rather doing it to give the former president the chance to be protected by the Supreme Federal Tribunal. After all, the country's highest court has the exclusive right to prosecute and sentence members of the executive and legislative branches, and thus a Cabinet post would put him beyond Moro's reach.

Noting that the investigations against the former president could be slowed in the top court, Neto suggested that was evidence Rousseff and Lula could be attempting to tamper with justice. With thousands of cases on its plate, the top court is in fact slow, but to use that as evidence of a crime was at best a dubious argument.

"The judge is not blind or deaf to what is happening," Neto wrote in the opinion published the day after the palace ceremony.[81] "Yesterday the whole country saw there is a clear intention of the former president, maybe even of the incumbent president, to intervene in the judicial

---

80. Daily *Folha de S.Paulo* took screen grabs of the judge's Facebook page and published an article about his participation in the rally on March 17, 2016.
81. The ruling was published by daily *Folha de S.Paulo* on March 17, 2016.

branch. That is unacceptable and cannot be allowed in any way."

Many were shocked by Neto's acknowledgment of political bias coupled with his contention that it had no impact on his legal rulings.

"I have shown my preference (for Rousseff's impeachment). This is my position as a citizen," said Neto. "I have as much right to exercise my citizenship as any Brazilian citizen, but that does not interfere in the judicial rulings I make. I decide according to the records, the facts that are proven or at least demonstrated in the case and according to the Brazilian judicial system."

In other times, a backlash by top judicial authorities against Neto would have been expected. But several hours after the ruling, some judicial pingpong aside, the upshot was that Lula still couldn't take office. Neto's decision was invalidated by appeals court judge Cândido Ribeiro. However, judge Regina Coeli Formisano then ruled on an injunction to keep Lula from taking office. Her decision was also scathing.

According to Formisano, there was an attempt to move cases against Lula to the Supreme Federal Tribunal because "seven of the 11 justices were appointed by the governing party."

"Indeed, such an assertion does not escape reality, as it was widely publicized in the national media that the intention of the president of the republic was precisely to 'shield' this citizen (Lula) and redirect Car Wash cases" to the Supreme Federal Tribunal, the judge wrote.[82]

The next day, that second injunction would also be knocked down by another judge. And so it went.

Brazil's judicial system has several layers, with the Supreme Federal Tribunal at the top. The next rung down is the Superior Tribunal of Justice, followed by regional federal courts and state courts.

Neto and the other federal court judges who followed him were not political appointees or elected by voters, as in many other countries.

---

82. The decision was published by news portal *G1* on March 17, 2016.

Instead, they had to pass a test to qualify as a judge, one of the most difficult positions to get in Brazil. The select group of more than 20,000 lower court federal judges can be of any political preference, gender or race, but historically the majority have been white men from states like São Paulo and Rio de Janeiro.[83]

Once in their positions, there is a lot of politics at play for ambitious judges who aspire to become "desembargadores," or top magistrates in each state. Rulings, connections and background all come into play with state governors and local heads of each court who pick "desembargadores." From there, they hope to be considered by presidents for high court appointments in Brasília, the Supreme Federal Tribunal being the greatest prize.

Still, even though politics are key at high levels in the courts, there are checks and balances. In a case like the dispute over Lula's nomination, when reaching the Supreme Federal Tribunal it's not for the chief justice to decide which member of the court gets to rule on the injunction. The country's top court has a lottery system to assure there is some balance in the number of cases for each justice, a strategy that arguably limits the ability of justices to interfere on behalf of politicians who might have had a hand in their appointments. As of this writing, however, the precise workings of the lottery process have never been revealed.

Rousseff and Lula had favorite justices to root for in the lottery. José Dias Toffoli was a former attorney for the Workers' Party and a former solicitor general under Lula. Ricardo Lewandowski spent much of his career in the city of São Bernardo do Campo, where the former president lived. Marco Aurélio Mello frequently sided with politicians in high-profile cases.

Luís Roberto Barroso had ruled months earlier to slow the impeachment proceedings and not allow the fast-track plan put forward by

---

83. News website *Nexo* published a survey of judges on Feb. 15, 2019.

Speaker Eduardo Cunha. The full court sided 8-3 with Barroso's decision, giving the president some breathing room to reorganize forces in Congress.

A justice seen as more neutral was also good enough for many members of the Workers' Party because of a simple calculus: In his ruling, Neto had essentially insulted the top court by calling it ineffective and slow. Rousseff aides believed that brashness would provoke some kind of reaction among justices aiming to protect the court's reputation.

In that vein, the man considered the father of the court for being the longest serving member, Celso de Mello, along with labor law specialist Rosa Maria Weber and moderate Cármen Lúcia, were the favorite picks of top members of the administration to decide on the case.

Even if those justices did not like the idea of having Lula as chief of staff or secretly wanted Rousseff to be impeached, the defense of the high court against a rebellious lower court judge could be a deciding factor.

Other members of the court could decide either way. Recently appointed Luiz Edson Fachin, who had openly endorsed Rousseff in the 2010 elections while a law professor, had ruled against the president on several occasions from the bench.

Teori Zavascki, who many observers considered to have the sharpest mind on the court, was the only justice with full access to Car Wash investigative documents, which could potentially mean he would be harsher against the top leaders of the deeply involved Workers' Party.

Luiz Fux, who had reportedly campaigned among politicians to get appointed by Rousseff, was a huge question mark.

Justice Gilmar Mendes was the only justice all but certain to rule against Lula. Appointed by center-right President Fernando Henrique Cardoso, Mendes had the conservative leanings common in most of Brazil's higher courts. Although he usually took the side of liberals in cases involving civil liberties, he often ruled against left-leaning parties in other areas.

So, the last thing that Rousseff's administration wanted was for Mendes to be named as the justice responsible for the ruling that would either keep the injunction blocking Lula or allow the president to have him as her chief of staff.

Mendes was the one picked in the lottery.

Rousseff's legal aides were disheartened, and with good reason. It took no more than a few hours for Mendes' decision to come out.

"The objective of the falsehood is clear: to stop an arrest warrant from a lower court judge from being carried out," Mendes said in his decision to keep Neto's ruling. "There was a scenario indicating that, in the next chapters, the former president could be implicated in previous investigations, arrested preemptively and criminally prosecuted. Taking office as a Cabinet minister would be a concrete way to block these consequences. The conversations intercepted with the authorization of the Curitiba court suggest that such was the purpose of the nomination."

Mendes had been an open critic of some of Moro's methods. However, no one in Brasília believed he would save his adversaries at a time impeachment looked more likely than ever thanks to the furor over the wiretap audios and growing revolt in Congress.

Meanwhile, the markets were celebrating, as a change of government looked more possible. The Bovespa, the flagship index of São Paulo's stock exchange, closed 6 percent up, the highest one-day jump since 2009.[84]

All that Rousseff could do was issue a statement saying Lula's nomination was "a private act of the president."

"Lula is not a defendant in any case and has no legal or constitutional barrier to occupy that position. The suits submitted to Justice Gilmar Mendes have no legal grounds that can attack the validity of Lula's nomination," the statement said.

Those words made no difference. While the full top court could have

---

84. News website *G1* wrote about this market spike on March 17, 2016.

considered Lula's appeal to annul Mendes' decision and reinstate him as chief of staff, it never did.

Lula could keep helping Rousseff from the outside, but the administration's ability to operate had undoubtedly been further compromised. The political maneuver aimed at saving the president from impeachment had the opposite effect: Now she was closer to being pushed out of the presidency.

CHAPTER 13

'Pronouncement
to the Nation'

It would be hard to believe anyone would record an explosive 15-minute audio on a messaging app and expect it to remain within closed circles. Even less so when the person recording it was a vice president who needed to introduce himself to many of his fellow citizens as the possible heir to the highest office of the land.[85]

So it caused chuckles when Michel Temer said that the recording made by him had been aimed at his party colleagues and was accidentally leaked. Regardless of how it got out, the audio, widely rebroadcast on April 11, 2016, helped Temer become a better-known figure before the key vote in Congress on Rousseff's fate.

"I want, at this moment, to speak to the Brazilian people," said the vice president in a serious tone. "Talk about some of the matters that must be faced by me. I do so with a lot of caution."

It was as if Rousseff's impeachment was a done deal. And at least in the court of popular opinion, it already was.

Six days before the lower chamber of Congress would vote on the impeachment legislation against Rousseff, 60 percent of Brazilians wanted her removed, according to a poll by the respected firm Datafolha.[86] That same poll found that nearly as many, 58 percent, also wanted Temer removed.

What did an even bigger majority want? A whopping 79 percent wanted new elections. That was wishful thinking; it was unimaginable that Temer would take office and then resign to make way for new elections.[87]

Six years earlier, Temer had almost been cut out of the winning presidential ticket. That was because of a corruption investigation that later gave origins to Car Wash and touched his political appointees in the port of Santos, outside São Paulo. Ten years earlier, he had barely garnered the minimum votes needed to keep his seat as a federal deputy.

---

85. The recording was widely distributed in the media. News magazine *Veja* was one of many to publish articles on it April 11, 2016.

86. The Datafolha poll was published in daily *Folha de S.Paulo* on April 9, 2016.

87. Temer reflects on his early years and being president in a book published in 2020, *A Choice. How a president managed to overcome a grave crisis and present an agenda for Brazil.*

When the impeachment push against Rousseff started gaining traction, it would have been easy for Temer to go down, too. After all, he was vice president, and the country's top electoral court was reviewing alleged campaign finance violations by the Rousseff-Temer campaign. And at first, there weren't many politicians outside the fractured PMDB who saw Temer as a solution. But the backroom dealmaker knew how to survive in politics, and now he was close to getting the biggest reward of his career.

Temer had already been called coup leader by Rousseff before the audio came out, which made him an even more disliked figure among his former left-leaning allies. But the recording also won him the attention of fellow conservative politicians and business leaders, even those who initially did not have reasons to support him, like Senate President Renan Calheiros and prominent members of Aécio Neves' PSDB.

In February, Temer's PMDB had already launched a pro-business government plan called "A Bridge to the Future," which was widely seen as part of the plan to kick the incumbent out of office and make Brazil's economy start running again with a lot of leeway for the private sector. The initiative, which included privatization of state assets and a reform of labor laws that would hit unions and halt gains for workers, was popular in market circles.

Few people on the streets knew Temer well, though. His earlier letter to Rousseff had quickly become a meme on Brazil's always very active social media channels. But many people, especially older people who made up a good number of protesters demanding Rousseff's removal, had little idea of what to expect of Temer.

Calling it his first "pronouncement to the nation," Temer said he chose to speak "now, when the Chamber of Deputies decides on an important vote to authorize the process of impeachment against madam president."

Temer said he had not spoken out the previous month so as not to give the impression he was "committing some act, practicing some gesture with a look toward occupying the place" of Rousseff. His decision to speak now, he said, was because many had asked that he give a "prelimi-nary word to the Brazilian nation."

The vice president then went on to broadly outline his goals if he became president. He would not, as he said critics claimed, cut social welfare programs like Bolsa Familia.

"That is a lie. It's false and the fruit of the most lowly form of politics that has taken over the country," he said.

Still, without providing details, Temer said reforms and "initial sac-rifices for the Brazilian people" would be necessary to jumpstart the economy, words that surely resonated among business leaders frustrated by Rousseff's response to the recession. Many thought she hadn't cut expenses enough.

Temer said the state "can't do everything." However, it should, he said, focus its efforts on security, healthcare and education, and then "turn the rest over to private enterprise," just as the program "A Bridge to the Future" suggested.

He also warned that in "three or four months everything would not be resolved," tempering short-term expectations while also laying the groundwork for what he wanted to do.

The political insider was shaping a new identity. Formerly a kingmaker rather than a king, who led a party historically known for its lack of politi-cal ideology, for its largesse and for doling out pork, Temer was positioning himself as a fiscally conservative budget trimmer ready to be the adult in the room in order to put Latin America's largest economy back on track.

But the economy would not be his only focus as president. Striking a conciliatory tone, Temer said his priority would be to bring peace to the fractured nation.

"The big mission is to pacify the country, unify the country," he said. "Whatever happens in the future, a government of national salvation, of national unification, is necessary. All parties must be willing to give their contribution to pull the country from the crisis. For that, we need dialogue."

The audio was proof that Temer wanted to facilitate that dialogue, but clearly only as president.

The day after the supposedly private remarks were broadcast nationally, Rousseff responded during a speech at the presidential palace, calling out Temer and lower house Speaker Eduardo Cunha.

"I am not sure who is the boss and who is the deputy boss," she said with a sarcastic tone and slight smirk, pausing a few seconds for applause from the audience.

As she continued, Rousseff's tone became serious, her words more forceful.

"One is the hand, not so invisible, which conducts the impeachment process with deviation of power and unimaginable abuse. The other scrubs his hands and rehearses the farce of the leak of an alleged inauguration speech," she said, standing in front of Brazilian flags.[88]

The recording, Rousseff said, "reveals the betrayal of me and of democracy."

By now, all of Brazil's political class was weighing in on Temer's recording, Rousseff's response to it and whether opponents had enough votes for impeachment.

"I can only say the following: If a conspiracy exists, it's from the people (who want Rousseff out)," Cunha told reporters in Congress the next day.

"We are committed, only and exclusively, with respecting the constitution," he added.

Sen. Romero Jucá from Temer's PMDB blasted Rousseff for her reaction to the audio. He said neither Temer nor anybody in Congress was taking any "deliberate action" against her but rather following the law.

"I am sorry that President Dilma is losing her serenity and trying to blame other people for the mistakes of her own government," he told

---

88. Rousseff's speech was played widely nationwide, including by news portal *G1* on April 13, 2016.

reporters. "If President Dilma wants to find people who screwed up the government, she should look within the government."

"I'm sorry she is losing her equilibrium," he said.

Sen. Humberto Costa from the Workers' Party had a different view. The audio, he said, proved that there was a "conspirator general of the Republic."

"Whether the audio was circulated intentionally or by accident, that speech shows a petty formula of disloyalty that the vice president has been using in the shadows, plotting to overthrow Dilma, someone who was twice his running mate," he said.

Temer appeared to be trying to stay above the fray, even though he himself was the cause of the latest ruckus. In an interview with GloboNews after Rousseff's response, Temer presented himself as a dedicated public servant ready to step up if he was called upon.

"I have a public life with a lot of experience. If destiny takes me to that function (the presidency) I'll be ready," he said.

And what if Rousseff beat the impeachment inquiry and remained in office? Temer smiled and said he would simply remain as vice president.

"I don't have anything to fear. I'll be at peace," he said.

In fact, things were moving in Temer's direction. Hours after his recording came out, a special commission of Brazil's lower house approved, 38 votes to 27, the motion to vote on Rousseff's impeachment in the chamber. The decision was widely expected weeks before and was mostly procedural. But the audio certainly gave it a push in the direction that the would-be future president wanted.

CHAPTER 14

'If I Lose'

For many Brazilians, staying home on Sunday to watch television is akin to a failed social life. The unwritten rule allows for exceptions whenever a big soccer match is on, especially during the World Cup. But April 17, 2016, was a different Sunday in the troubled nation, with many going to the beaches and streets early on to demonstrate either in favor of or against the impeachment of President Dilma Rousseff and then getting back to their couches for a long afternoon watching history unfold at the country's lower chamber in Congress.

In the capital Brasília, 300,000 people were expected to watch the impeachment vote on giant screens outside Congress, which prompted authorities to raise a metal barrier to separate protesters into two groups so there were no confrontations.[89] In the end, about 10,000 showed up.

Even if Rousseff got impeached in the Chamber of Deputies, which would require two-thirds of the 513 deputies voting in favor, that was only part way toward removing her. If the legislation prevailed there, it would then move to the Senate. If a simple majority of senators voted in favor, Rousseff would be suspended for up to 180 days. In that time period, the Supreme Federal Tribunal's chief justice would oversee a trial in the Senate. Rousseff would be removed only if two-thirds of the 81 senators voted in favor.

Despite the many steps, few political insiders believed Rousseff could remain in power if she lost that first vote. Rousseff herself appeared doubtful.

"If I lose (that first vote), I'm a card outside the deck," Rousseff told journalists a few days before the vote.[90]

By this point, many political insiders believed she could lose it. Party after party of her base had announced in prior days that they were no longer in her coalition, a step toward allowing their members to vote against her. Only hardcore leftists and some moderates publicly remained on her side.

The stakes could hardly have been higher that Sunday. Losing the vote would mean Rousseff's ally-turned-foe Michel Temer would be a step closer to becoming president. And for those on the left, Workers' Party supporters and Lula himself, something else was at stake: An eventual

89. An article published by news portal *G1* on April 17, 2016, presented the expectations for the day, including preparations for 300,000 to show up.
90. Rousseff was quoted by daily *Exame* on April 13, 2016.

ouster of Rousseff would mean Lula faced a bigger risk of jail time since there wouldn't be friends in the presidential palace to advocate for him with the country's top judges.

So, that Sunday morning many allies near the president were shocked to see her calmly get on her bike and go cycling.

"How can she be like that?" said one member of her public relations team. "I can't believe she stuck to her routine today."

Another ally said: "She has many flaws, but we can never deny that the old lady is brave. She knows she will lose; she was riding her bike for history."[91]

Brasília boils from Tuesday to Thursday, the only days Congress really works. On Sundays, the city is usually pretty dead. Planned by communist architect Oscar Niemeyer and inaugurated in 1960, the interior city of 2.5 million is home to hundreds of thousands of government workers. While sedate compared to the business hustle of São Paulo, and lacking in beauty compared to coastal Rio de Janeiro, Brasília is popular with many families because of its slower pace, cleaner streets and fewer signs of poverty (at least in the city center; there are large favelas on the periphery).

Parks and clubs are among the city's main attractions on weekends since cultural life is comparable to that of a countryside town, with few movie theaters and many activities organized around private homes.

Few big demonstrations are ever held in Brasília, probably in part because the esplanade in the middle of all the government buildings is so large that it's very difficult to fill with protesters.

Again, this particular Sunday was different. All the opposition's effort to oust Rousseff, going back to the end of the 2014 elections, and all the frustrations with Rousseff that many Brazilians had, were coming to

---

91. Both of these comments were made to AP's Mauricio Savarese, in Brasília to cover the vote, during off-the-record discussions.

the fore. At the same time, all the defensive moves the Workers' Party had made to hold on to the presidency until the end of a fourth term were at risk.

Rousseff's chances of survival had taken a turn for the worse two weeks before with a symbolic move. Temer's PMDB party, not known for breaking with any politician who provided a chance to wield power, decided after an executive meeting to do what House Speaker Eduardo Cunha suggested, and leave. Dropping from the president's coalition in Congress was not unanimous; Rousseff, though unpopular, still clung to some PMDB members in Rio de Janeiro and Minas Gerais states who wanted her to hold her office. But the top leaders of the kingmaking party had signaled they wanted her out so that Temer could take over.

As smaller centrist parties decided to do the same in the days before the impeachment vote, they did not express concern about the official accusations against Rousseff, such as the "fiscal maneuvering." Their leaders basically said there was no way to carry on in an administration that had little political support. The ship was sinking and no rat wanted to be on board when it went down.

The little boost Rousseff had gotten with Workers' Party supporters taking to the street also evaporated as she managed to keep only left-leaning parties in her coalition in Congress. That meant she had only one-fifth of the votes assured on her side. Was there any way she could stop the opposition from getting two-thirds of the Chamber of Deputies to vote against her?

Even if the chances of Rousseff's administration surviving were limited, there were still a few hands to be played. One of the liveliest places in Brazil's capital that weekend was a suite a few miles (kilometers) away from Rousseff's presidential residence. It was at the Royal Tulip hotel where Lula tried to persuade deputies to stay with Rousseff.[92]

---

92. Daily *Exame* reported on April 14, 2016, about meetings at the hotel.

The math was simple: If the opposition failed to get 342 votes out of 513 members, the president would remain in office. Any abstention would essentially count as a vote for the embattled leader.

Members of most parties represented in Congress met with the former president, according to press reports and statements the parties put out. Some lawmakers were interested in what Lula had to say and considered voting to keep the embattled Rousseff in office. Others accepted the meeting but did not show up.

Hardcore members of the Workers' Party who liked Rousseff hoped that the former president's charm gave them a fighting chance to survive. And Lula pulled out all the stops to try to keep his protégée from being impeached. In a final attempt to talk to as many Brasília insiders as possible, he barely slept during this stretch.

His question to all he met with was: "What's it going to take for you to stay with us?"[93]

Lula even talked to members of Temer's party who seemed to be somewhat split on the question. Most accounts Lula heard, however, were that Brazil was already under too much stress and that even if Rousseff survived the vote of that day, Cunha would authorize new impeachment legislation until he got what he wanted: Rousseff ousted and Temer as president.

Lula's closest allies had two lines of thought on what was at stake in the two potential outcomes.

One group believed that if Rousseff survived, the credit would go to Lula, who would get support from some adversaries to carry on as the de facto leader of the country in a Cabinet position. He would be less vulnerable to an arrest, and his popular touch could create a better political atmosphere until 2018, when he intended to run for the presidency. But

---

93. Daily *Folha de S.Paulo* reported on April 10, 2016, on Lula's meetings several days leading up to the lower house vote.

running in 2018 with Brazil's economy still struggling, which was very likely, could put his legacy at risk. How would it look if the man once Brazil's most popular politician lost a new run for the presidency?

A second camp believed Rousseff's downfall would put Lula at a bigger risk of going to jail and not even running in the 2018 elections. But they also saw the former president as a conciliator who could potentially be celebrated, when the time came, as a real option to unify Brazilians after so much fighting. They never imagined a man of his stature in jail and doubted the economic crisis would be over under Temer. When the time came, they hoped Lula would be called to the rescue. After all, there were no other leaders in Brazil with the same heft as Lula.

Detractors of the Workers' Party disagreed completely with both of these lines of thinking. Most wanted Rousseff impeached and ousted and Lula in jail or, at the very least, politically impaired. Although neither was a radical like Venezuela's late former President Hugo Chavez, they were clearly appealing more to their leftist base as impeachment and corruption investigations got closer to them.

Adversaries of the two main figures of the Workers' Party told business leaders over and over that once the two were out of the picture, uncertainties over Brazil's future would be gone and investors would flock back. Reforms would happen under Temer, and the Car Wash investigations would slow down, they believed.

Austerity measures would make investors trust Congress, and Temer would actually govern with a majority. That majority would be formed by right-leaning and centrist politicians, with a big chunk just trying to stay out of Judge Sergio Moro's sights. After some success in dragging the country out of the economic crisis, many of them thought it would be easy to keep the left-leaning parties far from the Palácio do Planalto in the 2018 presidential elections.

There was still risk that the 2014 Rousseff-Temer ticket would be annulled by Brazil's top electoral court on the campaign irregularities charges, many insiders noted. But they reasoned that if a new Temer administration managed to calm Brazil down and get support from investors, it would be likely that the court would rule the other way.

At last, these myriad what-if's and could-be's fell aside that Sunday afternoon — as the deputies' vote got under way.

After about 40 minutes of procedural discussions led by Cunha, Jovair Arantes, rapporteur of the impeachment legislation, presented what the commission had concluded and urged deputies to vote in favor of impeachment. Brazil was "sick," he said, and the only way forward was to push out Rousseff.

"This is the time for us to rewrite the democratic history of our country," said Arantes, from the conservative Brazilian Labor Party. "Brazil needs your vote."

"May God lead us," he said, concluding his speech.

God, it turned out, would get a lot of mentions by deputies on this day. The leader of the process, Cunha, was one who said he was looking for guidance from above.

Hours before the voting began, Cunha said he put on a gospel song by pastor Kleber Lucas — "God take care of me." Then he prayed "and gave everything that would happen that day to the hands of God," Cunha later recounted.[94]

Just as Rousseff and Lula had done all they could to convince legislators going into the vote, Cunha had shaped the process in ways he believed would help him. He put a buffet in his office for any legislators needing food. Many parties would bring in catering for their members; what Cunha offered was one more option for lawmakers to eat during

---

94. Cunha recounted this in his book, *Bye, Dear: A Diary of Impeachment*, published in April 2021.

the proceedings, thus encouraging them not to leave the building for meals.

Cunha didn't approve any lawmaker requests to leave the country for state-related travel over the 10-day period in April when he thought the vote most likely to happen, also canceling all government related engagements his office could influence. Finally, he structured the vote in a way that forced lawmakers to make a choice up front, eliminating ways for any hoping to hang back and see where the winds were blowing before voting.

In the 1992 impeachment vote against President Fernando Collor de Mello, there were two rounds of voting. Following congressional norms, votes happened one state at a time. For example, in that first round, all the members from the small state of Acre would vote, then the next state, and so on. Members who were not on the chamber floor to vote in the first round — because they were in the bathroom, having a meal or simply absent on purpose to avoid having to vote initially — got a chance to vote in the second round.

Cunha decided to do it differently. Voting would happen by state, but the second chance to vote for those absent would only occur right after their state had finished the first round of voting. Cunha would call any absent member again. Then he would move on to the next state. In other words, there would be no chance to wait for a second round and possibly cast a vote once the matter was decided.

Rousseff watched the voting unfold on television, first with Lula at the presidential residence and later by the side of her solicitor general, José Eduardo Cardozo, her staunchest defender in the legal arena.[95]

The rationale that many members of the Chamber of Deputies offered as they voted had little, if anything, to do with Rousseff's alleged crimes.

---

95. Daily *Folha de S.Paulo* reported on how Rousseff spent watching the lower chamber vote on April 19, 2016.

"I recognize the beautiful job that former President Lula did for Brazil, giving opportunities to the poor, who never got anything from previous administrations," said Adail Carneiro, from the progressive party Podemos, or We can. "I want to apologize to him, but I cannot reject the call of social media for us to give a new opportunity to the Brazilian people." He voted to impeach Rousseff.

Marco Feliciano, an evangelical preacher who had supported Rousseff in the 2010 elections and then switched to Neves in 2014, chose anti-left rhetoric. "With the help of God, for my family and the Brazilian people. For the evangelicals of all the country. Goodbye, dear," Feliciano said, mimicking how Lula, in the leaked audios, had called Rousseff "dear."

He added: "Goodbye to the Workers' Party, the party of darkness."

Valdir Colatto, a leader of lawmakers representing rural areas, gave a nod to his constituents. "For those Brazilians who were fooled by this administration, for our farmers who were tricked. If the farmers don't plant, no one eats," he said.

Others chose to celebrate the Car Wash investigation, putting the blame squarely on the left.

"For Sergio Moro!" said Hidekazu Takayama, an evangelical pastor from the Social Christian Party, who railed against "the thieves and the left."

A clown-turned-politician, Francisco Everardo Oliveira Silva, known as Tiririca, explained his vote for Rousseff's impeachment with a single sentence.

"I voted with heart and we'll have faith that Brazil will improve," Tiririca said.

As Rousseff calmly watched, she accepted some of the votes as part of the game and criticized former allies who turned on her. But one vote made her gasp.[96]

---

96. Rousseff recounted her shock at Bolsonaro's vote during an interview with AP's Mauricio Savarese in 2017.

'If I Lose'

Far-right Congressman Jair Bolsonaro stepped up to the microphone and began an explanation of the vote he was about to cast.

By this point, it was nearly a done deal that Rousseff would be impeached: 235 had voted in favor, compared to 82 against. But the words of Bolsonaro, known for provocative statements during a career in Congress that dated back to 1991, summed up how many conservatives were interpreting what was happening — and it had nothing to do with Rousseff's alleged breaking of laws.

"On this day of glory for the people there is a man who will go down in history. Congratulations, Speaker Eduardo Cunha," said Bolsonaro, receiving a few muddled cheers and boisterous boos.

"They lost in '64 and they lost now in 2016," said Bolsonaro, referring to the left and the beginning of the 1964-1985 dictatorship.

Surrounded by dozens of deputies, waving his hands and shouting into the microphone, Bolsonaro went on: "For the families and the innocence of children that the Workers' Party never respected! Against communism! For freedom! Against the São Paulo Forum!"

The São Paulo Forum, founded by the Workers' Party in its namesake city, is a conference of leftist parties and other groups from Latin America and the Caribbean — the kind of gathering that conservatives like Bolsonaro frequently bash. In recent decades, participants have mostly been fringe politicians of socialist leanings, but that is enough for the forum to be a bogeyman for far-right activists and fans of conspiracy theories.

Then came Bolsonaro's most fiery statement, which provoked gasps, boos and some muted cheers in the chamber as he delivered it: "In memory of Col. Carlos Alberto Brilhante Ustra, the dread of Dilma Rousseff!"

It was a shout-out to the military officer who had overseen the repressive apparatus that tortured Rousseff when she was imprisoned — clearly a low blow, and shocking even by Bolsonaro's standards.

In the early 1970s, Ustra was head of the Department of Operations and Information, an investigative unit of the Army that focused on gathering intelligence and torturing perceived enemies of the dictatorship. Dozens died while he ran the unit and several hundred were tortured. While in 2008 Ustra would be recognized as a "torturer" by a civil court in São Paulo, until his death in 2015 he continued to be active in military clubs, often defending the dictatorship.

Bolsonaro's hearty embrace of Ustra captured a growing idea in many circles, albeit a romantic and, for many, incorrect idea, that things were better when the military was in power. To hear Bolsonaro and supporters tell it, during the dictatorship there was less violence and less corruption in politics, and since things like gay marriage and LGBT rights didn't exist, they didn't endanger nuclear families made up of husbands and wives. According to this line of thinking, the only way to right the ship was to uproot leftist ideologies and bring back more "traditional values."

The thrice-married and dirty-mouthed Bolsonaro was hardly a model of the evangelical Christian values he espoused. His list of offensive statements was long: He said he would rather have a dead son than a gay son. During an argument, he told a congresswoman, "I wouldn't rape you because you don't deserve it." He frequently insulted gays, Blacks and women. But those kinds of statements, similar to the one about Rousseff's torturer, garnered him attention and added to an everyman persona.

"Brazil above everybody. God above everything. My vote is yes," Bolsonaro concluded his vote, cheers finally overtaking the boos as he raised his arms as if in victory.

What were Rousseff's thoughts and feelings as the far-right leader expressed himself in this way?

"Bolsonaro's vote was very sad to watch," Rousseff told The Associated Press in comments made a year later in an interview that still reflected the hurt. "I don't think average Brazilians are OK with what he said. Even those that didn't like me."

The voting continued. Others agreed with impeaching Rousseff but also wanted Cunha to pay for his crimes. "Today we are voting on Dilma's impeachment, but tomorrow it will be yours," said Expedito Netto from the Social Democratic Party. "Against corruption, wherever it comes from."

Some pro-Rousseff votes were also emotional.

"I am embarrassed to take part in this farce, this indirect election that is organized by a crook," said Jean Wyllys, a left-leaning gay lawmaker who had criticized Rousseff. "No to the coup!"

Some time after making his vote, Wyllys got close to Bolsonaro, a frequent foe in the chamber, and spit on him. Wyllys then turned away, pushing through the crowd of lawmakers on the chamber floor. All was caught on camera.

Luiz Sergio, a former Rousseff minister who had fallen out of favor with her, did not name his former boss when voting against her removal.

"Never in my life have I heard so many people use God's name in vain, as if He were a pamphlet," Sergio said. "In respect to the popular vote and democracy, I vote no."

One of the most emphatic no votes came from Glauber Braga, a member of the leftist Socialism and Democracy Party.

"The foundation of your presidency (of the chamber) smells like sulfur," he said, pointing at Cunha.

But these were in the minority. The overwhelming majority of deputies were against Rousseff. Some gave downright strange statements as they voted.

"Happy birthday to Ana, my granddaughter," said conservative Sergio Moraes.

Lawmaker Eder Mauro spread a fake news story in the chamber while voting in favor of impeachment.

"I, along with my children and my wife, form a family in Brazil. These criminals really want to destroy (the family) with propositions that children go through sex changes and learn about sex in school when they are 6 years old. So my vote is yes," Mauro said.

"For peace in Jerusalem, I vote yes," said moderate Ronaldo Fonseca.

Marcelo Álvaro Antônio, a close ally of Bolsonaro, went back up to the front after his "yes" vote, but not because he needed to do any further explaining.

"Just to correct one thing: I want to send a hug," he said. "I didn't mention my son, Paulo Henrique. Paulo Henrique, this is for you, son! A kiss!"

João Henrique Caldas, from the Brazilian Socialist Party, had an illogical rationale to support Rousseff's impeachment. "In Cuba, there are elections; in North Korea, there are elections; in Iraq, there are elections," he said, apparently arguing that holding elections, widely believed to be fraudulent in the countries he mentioned, doesn't necessarily mean there is true democracy.

"We can't turn our backs on public opinion and pretend that what the people say, what the streets say, don't matter at this moment," he added.

Gun control was also a reason to remove the president, according to Rogério Peninha Mendonça, an agronomist and member of Temer's PMDB.

"To amend the [gun-control] law, for our farmers and for the end of corruption in Brazil, I vote yes," he said.

Cabo Sabino, one of many policemen to become lawmakers in Brazil in recent years, chose to make fun of the president with an economic explanation for his vote.

"Dilma, you're feeling what all 10 million unemployed people felt when they lost their jobs. You are losing yours. Bye, dear. No need to come back," he said.

The reasoning of conservative Raquel Muniz was simply bizarre.

"My vote is a tribute to the victims of (highway) BR-251 and to say that Brazil has a solution, and that the mayor of Montes Claros shows that to everyone with his administration," she said. She was married to the mayor of Montes Claros, Ruy Muniz, who would be arrested the following day by federal police in a corruption scandal.

The vote that would be repeatedly played on newscasts was that of Speaker Cunha. He didn't even have to vote, since he was presiding over the session. But he chose to do so, as did then Speaker Ulysses Guimarães, also of PMDB, during the 1992 impeachment vote.

"May God have mercy on this nation. I vote yes," said Cunha, who simply sat back in his chair.

When the impeachment vote concluded, the final tally was 367-137 against Rousseff.

With the realization that she was now one step closer to being ousted, celebrations erupted among many congressmen, and fireworks flashed and echoed in many cities. Meanwhile, some deputies supporting Rousseff cried in the chambers.

Many Brazilians believed the demise of Rousseff and her Workers' Party would mean the start of the country's comeback. Even though it meant little-known Temer could soon take over, many hoped that Rousseff's ouster would lead to a massive cleaning out that would sweep away Temer, Cunha and many others. Others likely just pretended they believed that.

For many who watched the proceedings live — whether one supported impeaching Rousseff and felt elated relief or thought it a terrible idea and felt dejected — another common feeling at the conclusion was embarrassment. The voting had laid bare the lack of preparation and seriousness of many congressmen. Beyond that, there was the reality that many deputies were themselves accused of crimes and thus were hardly in a position to judge anybody.

CHAPTER 15

'Bye, Dear'

"Mixed up in all this is a degree of prejudice against women," Rousseff told foreign journalists on April 19, 2016, a few days after the Chamber of Deputies impeached her. "There are attitudes towards me that would not exist with a male president."

In the months leading up to that vote, Rousseff and supporters had often noted that men — that is, male former presidents — did some of the same accounting maneuvers Rousseff was accused of and faced no consequences.

In the weeks between the Chamber of Deputies vote and when the

Senate would take up the legislation, arguments that misogyny was a leading factor in impeachment were increasingly being articulated by Rousseff supporters and debated nationally.

Sexist chants had been heard at some anti-Rousseff rallies, and that was far from the first time. During the opening ceremony of the World Cup in 2014, many could be heard chanting, "Hey Dilma, take it in the ass!"

In 2015, stickers appeared of Rousseff with superimposed spread legs; online vendors stopped selling them after a public outcry that included the government lodging complaints with the Ministry of Justice and the Attorney General. José Eduardo Cardozo, the president's top legal adviser, said several investigations were opened related to sexism against the president, but none amounted to legal action against any of the alleged perpetrators.

The atmosphere was clearly hostile, but was Brazil's first woman president really being submitted to an impeachment push because of machismo? And if having a woman president really was so problematic, how was it that twice the nation voted one into office?

Women have long been a minority in Congress; in 2016, they held only 11 percent of the 594 seats in the Chamber of Deputies and Senate. But it wasn't as if Rousseff was the first woman to hold an important political office in Brazil or aspire to the top office in the land.

Before Rousseff was elected, women had served as governors in the states of Rio de Janeiro and Rio Grande do Sul, among others. São Paulo had elected two female mayors, Luiza Erundina and Marta Suplicy. And Marina Silva, environmental minister during Lula's presidency, competed against Rousseff in the 2010 and 2014 presidential elections.

As always with gender issues, nuance was important. Though Rousseff's Cabinets did have more women than those of previous administrations, she had always presented herself as a leftist president for all Brazilians. Her agenda was not heavily focused on the rights of women, racial minorities, members of the LGBT community or labor unions, all groups that tended to vote for left-leaning leaders and often supported the Workers' Party. But it wasn't lost on her that she was the first woman (and a woman divorcee) to be president in a nation with deep religious, conservative and sexist currents — and she saw that as a great responsibility.

"By the sovereign decision of the people, today will be the first time that a presidential sash will be fastened to the shoulder of a woman," Rousseff said at the beginning of her inaugural speech on Jan. 1, 2011, pausing for several seconds so many in Congress could stand up and cheer loudly. Later that day, when the presidential Rolls-Royce paraded through Brasília, Rousseff rode with her daughter, Paula. Her predecessors had always been accompanied by their wives.

In that first inaugural speech, which lasted 40 minutes, several times Rousseff mentioned women, from her hope that her presidency would lead to other women presidents to arguing that Brazil could only move forward with the full participation of women in all aspects of life. She also used a word, "presidenta," which prompted grammarians to weigh in on its correctness. Her use of the word, and by extension a request that she be referred to with it, was something that some male critics, major media companies and even some allies openly ignored.

In Portuguese the word for president is "presidente." The spelling of the noun itself doesn't change whether the person being referred to is male or female. Gender is defined by the article in such words, so a male president would be "um presidente," and a female president "uma presidente." The definite article works the same, so "the (male) president" is "o presidente" and "the (female) president" is "a presidente." It was common for news organizations to say Rousseff would be "A primeira presidente do Brasil," "The first female president of Brazil."

Many nouns and adjectives in Portuguese, a Romance language, do change their ending depending on gender. For example, a male nurse is an "enfermeiro" and a female nurse is an "enfermeira." But some words like "presidente" are considered gender neutral.

Rousseff had said "presidenta" on the campaign trail in 2010, so the linguistic debate was well underway. Grammarians generally agreed that her use of the word was grammatically acceptable though not common or linguistically necessary. Detractors made a play on the word, making it "presi*danta*." "Anta" in Portuguese literally means tapir but can also mean somebody very stupid.

Using the word "presidenta" in her first speech as president, Rousseff was emphasizing that gender mattered, that she would be a different president in part because she was a woman.

Fast forward back to impeachment.

For many feminists, the use of the phrase "Tchau, querida," or "Bye, dear," during the Chamber of Deputies vote, was derogatory. Many legislators chanted the phrase and waved signs with it during the entire process.

On the surface, legislators were simply copying, with a good dose of irony, what Lula had said to Rousseff at the end of their wiretapped conversation about the details of his becoming her chief of staff. But the ferocity and frequency of its use made it feel like something beyond just a playful goodbye; Rousseff, the nation's first woman president, was being removed from the public space.

"When someone who likes us says that, it's one thing," Carol Patrocinio, a São Paulo based communications specialist who often blogs about issues related to women, wrote on Medium the day after the impeachment vote. "But when somebody tells us that in other moments every woman knows what that 'dear' means. And it isn't pretty."

In her post, titled "What is behind the 'Bye, dear' of pro-impeachment deputies?" Patrocinio argued the phrase was used as a way to put women in their place and was used in ways that had several other meanings.

"That dear could be swapped out for easy, vagabond, slut, bitch, crazy, hysterical, manic and many other adjectives that are usually used only when referring to women," she wrote.[97]

Indeed, Rousseff had been called some such names going back to the 2013 protests against her administration. The impeachment saga had been no different.

In early April, less than two weeks before the lower chamber vote, magazine *IstoÉ* put out a story that turned heads, and in many circles was roundly criticized for allegedly being sexist. *IstoÉ* was one of Brazil's least read magazines and by no means a reflection of how Brazilian media treated Rousseff. Still, its covers and headlines, sometimes outlandish, got attention.

"Nervous Explosions of the President," read the title on the cover, which also featured a photo of Rousseff apparently yelling.[98]

Rousseff said she believed that cover photo had actually been taken months before when she was attending a soccer game and celebrating a goal by the national team.

"*IstoÉ*'s coverage of me was filled with insults and lies," Rousseff said during an interview, adding that the aim of the cover was to make her look hysterical.

The article, citing mostly anonymous sources in the presidential palace, painted a picture of a president both fuming at enemies and out of touch with what was happening in a country suffering both political and economic crises. There were instances when Rousseff allegedly broke furniture in a rage, shouted at aides, and generally was irritable, irascible and unapproachable. Much of the description was in line with what aides and several media reports had said about Rousseff during her first term: she was a tough boss, didn't suffer fools and was

---

97. The blog post was published April 18, 2016.
98. The *IstoÉ* cover was published April 6, 2016.

quick to lay into aides or other staff when they did or said anything she disapproved of.

The *IstoÉ* piece made the case that Rousseff had not come to terms with the reality that she could be removed from office. It even went so far as to recap the five stages of grieving when a loved one dies: denial, anger, adjustment, depression and finally acceptance. Rousseff, the piece argued, was vacillating between denial and anger.

In closing, a parallel was made between Rousseff's rule and that of Maria I, Portugal's queen from 1777 to 1816. Brazil was a colony under the Portuguese crown and in the early 19th century Maria moved to Brazil. While seen as a competent ruler early in her reign, during much of her adult life she suffered mental illness, thus the nickname "Maria a Louca," or "Maria the Crazy."

"It is not just in our time or our current circumstances that, on the verge of losing power, government officials act in a crazy way and start to deny reality," said *IstoÉ*, transitioning from Rousseff's alleged detached moments to a recap of some of Queen Maria's craziest documented moments.

There were plenty of examples of male leaders in Brazil's history losing control, whether because of mental illness or dictatorial ways, unleashing violence on the population. That the article picked Maria a Louca underscored for many that Rousseff's gender was being attacked. The only other president to be impeached in Brazil's modern history, Fernando Collor de Mello, had a personality much more overtly aggressive than Rousseff's. However, the media portrayal of Collor during his impeachment saga in 1992 was of a corrupt politician who had been abandoned by allies because of a failing administration, not because of his temper.

Rousseff, speaking about the *IstoÉ* story, told a roundtable of journalists days after the Chamber of Deputies impeachment vote that "it says the following: a woman under pressure has to be hysterical, nervous and unstable. And they don't accept that I'm not nervous, hysterical or unstable."

Carlos José Marques, *IstoÉ*'s editorial director, in media interviews brushed off suggestions that the report had been sexist.

"If it had been about a male president, how would they rate it?" he told BBC World. "As a feminist cover because a man is on it? Obviously not."[99]

One area in which vulgarities and overt sexism toward Rousseff could sometimes be masqueraded as political criticism was in memes, practically a Brazilian national pastime. Shared on WhatsApp and other social media platforms at fast speeds, doctored videos and photos, plays on words or mangled quotes taken out of context, memes are equal opportunity offenders. No politician, actor, musician, athlete or institution is ever fully exempt. But during the impeachment process, some memes about Rousseff went beyond playful or even harsh and instead were dehumanizing and even violent.

Consider a handful of the memes:

— In 2016 on Facebook, a picture of Rousseff looking straight into the camera was placed next to a picture of an apparent witch with the phrase below: "Everybody gets the witch they deserve."
— In the days after Rousseff tried to name Lula her chief of staff, on Facebook a doctored picture of Lula appeared with a wig like Rousseff's hair and the red business suit she would wear, with the title "A presidento." The implication was clear: Lula, a man, was going to truly be the president.
— During impeachment, side-by-side images appeared on WhatsApp and Facebook of Rousseff and Marcela Temer, the wife of Vice President Michel Temer. On the left was the naked backside of a cartoonish Rousseff with wide hips and fat rolls, and on the right was Marcela Temer, the former beauty pageant contestant many years

---

99. Interview with BBC World published April 18, 2016.

the junior of Rousseff, looking sexy and elegant. "For Marcela Temer, I vote yes," said the meme's text.

— During impeachment, several memes showing Rousseff beat up, sometimes in cartoon fashion and sometimes with manipulated photos. "The light I see at the end of a tunnel was a train," read the text of a meme with a doctored photo of bruised and bloodied Rousseff.

In a paper titled "Gender and humor on social media: the campaign against Dilma Rousseff in Brazil," three researchers analyzed 69 memes about Rousseff between 2014 and 2016.

The memes were not all gender-based, but those with a basis in misogyny had a role in shaping the public's view of the process to remove Rousseff, the researchers concluded.

"Those stereotypes were part of the public campaign to socially legitimize the coup against Rousseff, giving a certain prominence on social media," they wrote. [100]

While it would be impossible to fully measure what role sexism had in pushing impeachment forward, one thing was clear: Many women deputies had not been moved by a feeling of gender solidarity when it came to casting their votes.

Of the 49 women deputies voting, 29 favored impeachment and 20 were against.[101]

100. The analysis was published by Fagner Carniel, Lennita Ruggi and Júlia de Oliveira Ruggi in 2018.
101. *Brasil de Fato* news portal did a count on April 18, 2016.

CHAPTER 16

Suspended

As the impeachment proceedings moved from the raucous lower house, where backbenchers had clearly followed Speaker Eduardo Cunha's lead, to the more subdued Senate, Dilma Rousseff's prospects hardly improved.

Rousseff would be suspended if a simple majority voted in favor. While she had more support in the Senate than in the Chamber of Deputies, it was widely expected that at least half of the 81 senators would vote to suspend her. If that happened, then the Senate would have up to 180 days to conduct a trial, overseen by the chief justice of the Supreme Federal

Tribunal, for a final vote on removal. In the meantime, Temer would take over as interim president.

This vote, on May 12, 2016, clearly represented a major event, but Brazilians reacted with a mix of disdain and apathy, as if it had already been factored in for months. There had also already been a good bit of impeachment-related drama the week leading up to the vote, so some fatigue had surely settled in.

First, Speaker Cunha, who just the month before had guided impeachment legislation through the Chamber of Deputies, was removed from his seat by Supreme Federal Tribunal Justice Teori Zavascki. While this had been expected to happen sooner or later because of the strength of the corruption allegations against him, it was still a dramatic development. Rousseff supporters couldn't help but wonder (and get angry when thinking about) what might have happened had Cunha been removed sooner.

Then a few days later, Waldir Maranhão, Cunha's successor as speaker, shockingly declared the Chamber of Deputies' impeachment vote annulled because of alleged irregularities, such as party leaders telling members how to vote.

Deputies "should have been able to vote freely and according to their personal convictions," Maranhão, a member of the right-leaning Progressive Party, said in a statement explaining why he invalidated the vote.

The decision had a questionable legal basis. Upon hearing the news, Rousseff told supporters she needed more information and urged caution. Within 24 hours, the criticism was so intense that Maranhão had reversed himself.

Two days later, senators were debating Rousseff's future during a session that lasted more than 20 hours.

"Bleary-eyed legislators gathered in the early hours of the morning to cast their electronic vote," National Public Radio's Lulu Garcia-Navarro said when the vote finally happened.

Not even the most hardcore supporters of the former guerrilla-fighter-turned politician expected her to avoid suspension. The low energy that day felt like a hangover compared to the highly charged atmosphere of the previous months.

Brazilian politicians, not unlike many around the world, are known for being long-winded. And there is always reelection to think about. What better place to record pithy statements for future television ads than the Senate floor while making a decision that would alter the course of the nation? It didn't really matter if people were tuning in at that moment.

Starting on Wednesday and going into the wee hours of the following day, every senator got 15 minutes to explain how they would vote, which didn't include the time between each speech or clarifying procedural questions. By midnight, 15 hours into the debate, only 40 of the 70 senators scheduled to speak had done so. At one point, Senate President Renan Calheiros appealed to senators to only take 10 minutes each, leading to sharp rebukes by Workers' Party senators who said they would not have their freedom of speech curtailed. But even Calheiros, whose people skills had helped him survive several corruption scandals, was losing his cool.

"I'm asking for everybody's patience because we need to see this through to the end," he said at one point, clearly frustrated.

Outside, several thousand supporters and opponents of impeachment had gathered in front of the Senate. The crowds were notably smaller than those that came for the lower house vote, which was on a Sunday. Just as for the lower chamber vote, during the Senate proceedings supporters and detractors outside were kept on opposite sides of a wall that split the lawn.

Minor clashes broke out between Rousseff supporters and police, who shot pepper spray in response to firecrackers and rocks thrown at them. Emergency workers took several people away.

Suspended

In stark contrast to the carnivalesque atmosphere of the lower house vote, there was little cheering or jeering inside the Senate chamber. Most senators were former governors, mayors of big cities or veteran parliamentarians, which assured a more subdued and statesmen-like approach to debating and voting. As expected, the arguments for Rousseff's removal were more focused, with some senators even lamenting what they were about to do.

"Everybody here is broken-hearted. We don't want to do this, but it's unavoidable," said Marcelo Crivella, a senator from Rio de Janeiro who was also a gospel singer and bishop for the powerful evangelical Universal Church of the Kingdom of God. One year before, Crivella had been Rousseff's fisheries minister.

"Brazil has come to a stop since last year," Crivella said, while adding that in her life Rousseff had done "a good job" for Brazil's young democracy.

Sen. Magno Malta, like many senators about to judge Rousseff, was dogged by a long list of scandals that included allegations of embezzlement, nepotism and bribes. That baggage didn't stop him from describing the country as being plagued by an illness that had to be removed. Malta had grown up in politics as an ally of the Workers' Party. But as he garnished more evangelical votes and focused on an anti-pedophilia agenda, he had become closer to far-right presidential hopeful Jair Bolsonaro.

"To improve the life of the nation right now we need to remove them (the Workers' Party)," Malta told journalists outside the Senate floor during an interval. "We will start to breathe again, and the doctor will say the nation has given signs of life and will be stable soon."

Despite a more somber tone, most spent little time actually litigating whether Rousseff had committed a crime or deserved to be removed for the kind of budget maneuvering that previous administrations had also done.

Former footballer-turned-senator Romário de Souza Faria, who started his career as a Rousseff ally and member of the Brazilian Socialist Party, called impeachment "a bitter medicine" that he would ultimately vote for.

"It isn't easy to be president, but anyone who sits on that chair needs to be aware of their responsibilities. They can't say they didn't know or blame their subordinates," the 1994 World Cup winner and Barcelona legend said, without touching the accusation against the president.

Vanessa Grazziotin, a senator of the Communist Party of Brazil, who would vote against suspending Rousseff, said lawmakers wanted to remove the president to block corruption investigations.

"They think she was not strong enough to stop Car Wash. Now they trick the population with the objective of selling illusions, as if jobs were coming back and graft will be finished," she said. "They want to take her place to once again use the old neoliberal policies. That is why we will oppose this new administration from the start."

Before voting for Rousseff's suspension, Sen. Fernando Collor de Mello, a former president who was impeached in 1992 by the Chamber of Deputies for corruption and resigned before the Senate could vote, argued his own impeachment saga was more rigorous.

"In 1992, in an analogous process, less than four months was enough between the presentation of the accusation and the decision to resign," said Collor, presenting himself as somebody who courageously decided to step down, though notably leaving out any mention of the influence peddling scheme he was accused of. "In the current process, eight months have already passed. Depending on the result of today's judgement, another six months are expected before the final judgment. The ritual (of impeachment) is the same, but the rhythm and the rigor are not."

When at last the drawn-out speechmaking concluded and the final vote was announced, there was little cheering.

Rather matter-of-factly, the Senate voted 55-22 to suspend Rousseff from office, putting a hard stop to her time at the Palácio do Planalto after five years and five months.

Suspended

News of the vote came as the world's eyes were already focused on Brazil, with the Summer Olympics in Rio de Janeiro just a few months away. Would the political turmoil have an impact? The International Olympic Committee moved quickly to assuage any such fears.

"There is strong support for the Olympic Games in Brazil, and we look forward to working with the new government to deliver successful Games in Rio this summer," IOC President Thomas Bach said in a statement put out shortly after the vote.

The Aug. 5-21 games, the statement said, "have now entered into a very operational phase, and issues such as these have much less influence than at other stages of organizing the Olympic Games."

In the weeks before the Senate suspended Rousseff, she had veered further left in speeches at the presidential palace in front of crowds that appeared to have renewed passion for her, sometimes chanting that she was "a warrior of the Brazilian people." Those feisty speeches sounded a lot like the rhetoric she used during the 2014 campaign.

University students, land reform and LGBT rights activists, among other progressives, flocked to Brasília in the days before the vote. In a sense, the festive events were a way for Rousseff to say goodbye.

Through it all, she showed her tough side.

"I'm not afraid of fighting," Rousseff told a group of activists promoting women's rights a few days before the Senate vote.[102]

But in the hours after the suspension vote, few staunch Rousseff supporters were outside Congress. The pressure on the streets of major cities was far from the levels at the beginning of the year. Like the senators who had just voted, many local media outlets spent little time re-litigating the case against Rousseff. Instead, they were focusing on Temer's liberalizing program for the near future, hoping it would drag Brazil out of its economic crisis. Much of his plan had already been revealed, albeit

---

102. Rousseff was quoted in a *New York Times* article published May 11, 2016.

169

in a camouflaged way, in PMDB's recently announced plan, "A Bridge to the Future."

The outcome of the Senate vote was announced shortly after dawn in a silent Brasília, as if winners didn't want to boast and losers were too sorry to keep crying foul on that day.

Most Rousseff official portraits had already been removed from executive branch offices. Her desk at the presidential palace had been cleared.

Rousseff arrived at 9 a.m. at the palace to prepare her goodbye speech. She would speak shortly after receiving the official notification to leave the office around 11 a.m.

"What is at stake with this impeachment process is not only my term. What is at stake is the respect of the ballots, the sovereign will of the Brazilian people and the constitution," she said, with ministers, lawmakers and hardcore supporters at her side. "Since I was reelected, part of the opposition asked for a vote recount, tried to annul the elections and then openly conspired for my impeachment. They sank Brazil into a permanent state of political instability, stopping the economy's recovery. Their sole intent was to take by force what they couldn't get in the polls."

Referring, as she often did, to being brutalized during the dictatorship, Rousseff continued: "I already suffered the unspeakable pain of torture. The affliction of cancer. And now I suffer once more the indescribable pain of injustice. What hurts the most at this moment is to understand I am a victim of a judicial and political farce.

"I fought all my life for democracy. I confess I never thought I would have to fight again against a coup in my country."

With that, she left the Palácio do Planalto through the front door. On Jan. 1, 2011, Rousseff had walked up a ramp leading to the palace. She decided not to traverse the same path when leaving, as administration officials worried that symbolically that would signal her presidency was over.[103] Technically, though suspended, her political fate still rested on one more Senate decision, which would come after a trial overseen by the chief justice of the Supreme Federal Tribunal.

Outside was a crying Lula, surrounded by supporters. Dressed in a light blue collared shirt, not the usual Workers' Party red that he often wore during symbolic events, the former president had nothing to say about what had taken place. As he walked away, he told journalists simply, "Now I am going home."

Meanwhile, a smiling Rousseff calmly greeted those outside the presidential palace. Sweating in her white jacket, at 11:41 a.m. she finally reached the car that would take her to the nearby Palácio da Alvorada, the presidential residence. She would be able to stay there until a final decision on her presidency was reached. About 30 aides also went to the presidential residence, the suspended president's last trench, to plan the resistance and begin attacking the new administration.

Though Rousseff still had one more chance to keep her job, her capabilities were greatly reduced. She still had the presidential residence, but other trappings of power, including use of the presidential plane, were already Temer's.

The conversation was not about her any longer.

---

103. Daily O *Globo* reported two days before her suspension on discussions about how she would exit the palace.

Impeachment, December 2015 to August 2016

A demonstrator with his face painted the colors of the Brazilian flag is seen in São Paulo on Dec. 13, 2015, during a protest in favor of impeaching President Dilma Rousseff. In general, Brazilians calling for Rousseff's ouster would wear national colors and take flags to protests. (AP Photo/Andre Penner)

Demonstrators against impeaching President Dilma Rousseff are seen marching in São Paulo on Dec. 16, 2015. The large green sign in the front, which reads "Não ao golpe," or "No to the coup," was one of the central rallying cries of Rousseff and supporters, who argued the impeachment process was illegitimate. (AP Photo/Andre Penner).

Protestors calling for President Dilma Rousseff's impeachment parade with large inflatable dolls of Rousseff and former President Luiz Inácio Lula da Silva in São Paulo on March 13, 2016. While the accusations of budget maneuvering that were the basis of the impeachment legislation against Rousseff had no connection to Lula, and various corruption cases against Lula had no connection to Rousseff, many Brazilians, from pro-impeachment protesters to lawmakers, would lump the two together to argue that the leftist Workers' Party was corrupt and needed to be removed from power. (AP Photo/Andre Penner)

Several lawmakers, including Congressman Jair Bolsonaro, seen second from left in the front row, celebrate in Brasília on April 11, 2016, after a committee vote to advance the impeachment legislation to the full lower Chamber of Deputies. The chamber would vote on it less than a week later. (AP Photo/Eraldo Peres)

Former President Luiz Inácio Lula da Silva, mentor of President Dilma Rousseff, holds a rally against impeachment in Rio de Janeiro on April 11, 2016. Throughout the entire impeachment process, Lula would advocate for Rousseff and try to keep her in power. (AP Photo/Leo Correa)

Police are seen guarding Congress in Brasília on April 16, 2016, as lawmakers debate and prepare to vote on impeachment legislation against President Dilma Rousseff. High tensions around impeachment meant a large law enforcement presence during votes. (AP Photo/Felipe Dana)

Speaker Eduardo Cunha, seen sitting in the center of the table, leads the debate on whether to impeach President Dilma Rousseff on April 16, 2016. Meanwhile, many lawmakers in favor of impeachment hold signs saying "Tchau, Querida," or "Bye, Dear," which were directed at Rousseff. (AP Photo/Eraldo Peres)

Pro-government demonstrators in Brasília watch a screen as lawmakers vote on impeachment on April 17, 2016. Because of high tensions, pro- and anti-government protestors were separated by a large fence during voting in the Chamber of Deputies. (AP Photo/Felipe Dana)

Protestors calling for the ouster of President Dilma Rousseff watch on a big screen in Rio de Janeiro as lawmakers in Brasília vote on impeachment legislation on April 17, 2016. Impeachment proceedings were televised nationally, which allowed people in all corners of Brazil to tune in. (AP Photo/Silvia Izquierdo)

President Dilma Rousseff holds a news conference in Brasília on April 18, 2016, the day after the Chamber of Deputies voted to impeach her and move the process to the Senate. While comparatively Rousseff enjoyed broader supporter in the Senate than in the lower chamber, losing that first vote significantly increased the chances she would be removed. (AP Photo/Eraldo Peres)

President Dilma Rousseff lights a torch next to Olympic volleyball player Fabiana Claudino during a ceremony at the presidential palace in Brasília on May 3, 2016. At this point, Rousseff had been impeached by the Chamber of Deputies, but the Senate was still more than a week away from voting on whether to suspend the president and put her on trial. The impeachment process happened during the runup to the Summer Olympics, which were hosted by Rio de Janeiro and would begin on Aug. 5, 2016. (AP Photo/Eraldo Peres)

President Dilma Rousseff greets supporters as she leaves the presidential palace after the Senate voted to suspend her on May 12, 2016. After the vote, Rousseff blasted the impeachment process and promised to continue fighting what she characterized as an injustice more painful than the torture she endured during the military dictatorship. (AP Photo/Felipe Dana)

Michel Temer, who had been vice president to President Dilma Rousseff, arrives at the presidential palace on May 12, 2016, after the Senate voted to suspend Rousseff and put her on trial for alleged violations of fiscal law in managing the federal budget. The Senate's vote made Temer the interim president. In his first speech, he promised pro-market reforms and an end to the paralysis in Congress. (AP Photo/Felipe Dana)

Demonstrators gather on Copacabana Beach in Rio de Janeiro on July 31, 2016, to demand the removal of President Dilma Rousseff. At this point, Rousseff had been suspended, her vice president, Michel Temer was interim president, and the Senate was preparing to begin the final trial in August, which was when the Rio de Janeiro Summer Olympics were to kick off. (AP Photo/Silvia Izquierdo)

Supporters of President Dilma Rousseff demonstrate in São Paulo on Aug. 29, 2016, as the Senate conducts the final trial of Rousseff. Protestors in the front hold a sign that says "Fora Temer," or "Out with Temer." As it became increasingly likely Rousseff would be removed, supporters were upping their calls for the ousting of interim President Michel Temer, who had been Rousseff's vice president. (AP Photo/Andre Penner)

Workers at the Ministry of Transparency, Supervision and Control use brooms to scrub the door of Minister Fabiano Silveira and call for his resignation after a recording emerged of Silveira advising lawmakers targeted by the Car Wash investigation into kickbacks to politicians and other officials. Silveira, who would resign, had been appointed by interim President Michel Temer just two weeks before. This was one of several scandals to emerge during the first weeks of Temer's administration. (AP Photo/Eraldo Peres)

The tally of senators' vote on permanent removal of President Dilma Rousseff is seen on a big screen in the chamber on Aug. 31, 2016. By 61-20, the Senate decided that Rousseff should be removed from office. Michel Temer would finish her term, and for the first time since 2003 the Workers' Party no longer occupied the presidency. (AP Photo/Eraldo Peres)

CHAPTER 17

All White Men

It was nearly noon on May 12, 2016, when Michel Temer officially became Brazil's interim president. The process was straightforward: He needed only to sign a few documents shortly after lawmakers suspended Rousseff.

Globo Television aired a short video of Temer taking care of the paperwork and then shaking hands with several white men, middle-aged to elderly, all in suits and ties. It was a striking image compared to Rousseff and her entourage, which always included women, people of color and youth. It would also be a sign of what was to come with Temer's Cabinet.

A few hours later, Temer was sworn in during an 11-minute ceremony in the Senate. But those initial glimpses of the interim president would not be the most memorable of the day. It was 4:03 p.m. at the presidential palace when Temer appeared in the ceremonial room to swear in 22 members he had picked for his Cabinet. Most were from his PMDB party, and they had much else in common: Again, all were white men, and at least one-third were being investigated in the sprawling Car Wash probe.

It marked the first time since the 1974-1979 government of Gen. Ernesto Geisel that there were no women ministers.

The problem, newly minted Chief of Staff Eliseu Padilha said the day after Temer took office, was that parties that were part of the governing coalition had not put forward female candidates for ministry posts.

"We tried various ways, in terms of availability and roles, to find women," he told news portal G1, adding that the government would encourage parties to put forward female candidates.

For many Brazilians, it was as if leaders of this new administration said they didn't know any women.

In addition to Padilha, who whipped votes for impeachment after leaving Rousseff's Cabinet in December,[104] Temer's long-time friend Geddel Vieira Lima, also a former member of the previous administration, was appointed secretary of government, with the special role of representing the president before lawmakers.

Temer had prizes for every party that helped him get the new job. That included leading figures of the right-leaning PSDB, once a center-left group that broke away from PMDB in the late 1980s because of corruption allegations. One of the PSDB members who had pushed hardest for the creation of the party was Sen. José Serra, who became foreign minister of the interim administration. Serra had lost his second presidential election to Rousseff in 2010.

---

104. Padilha's role in whipping votes for Temer was widely reported from the time impeachment proceedings began.

Deputy Bruno Araújo, deemed a future leader of the PSDB, was named minister of cities, a role focused on the federal government's intersection with mayors.

Sen. Blairo Maggi, a farming magnate who had the dubious distinction of having received Greenpeace's "Golden Chainsaw" award in 2005 for destruction of the Amazon, was appointed agriculture minister.

Marcos Pereira, a lawyer and evangelical bishop in the powerful pentecostal Church of the Kingdom of God, became industry and trade minister.

Temer picked as his economy minister Henrique Meirelles, a man Lula had repeatedly pitched to Rousseff for the position, though she never heeded the recommendation. Meirelles was Brazil's central bank governor for all eight years of Lula's presidency.

Temer confidant Wellington Moreira Franco did not get a role immediately, reportedly because he needed some time off. But two weeks later, the man seen as the president's right hand would be put in charge of an ambitious privatization program.

Finally, there was also room for a politician Rousseff has refused to talk about publicly: Gilberto Kassab, the head of Social Democratic Party, and once a friend of hers. A backroom dealmaker like Temer, moderate and soft spoken Kassab was a minister and an advisor during Rousseff's administrations.

Before the impeachment process began, media reports suggested Rousseff and Kassab had been plotting to make his party stronger in Congress by weakening Temer's PMDB. That, the thinking went, would weaken the impeachment process against Rousseff. When Temer became president, many were shocked to learn that Kassab was named minister for technology and communication. The betrayal was evident.

"It is not worth it to talk about him," Rousseff said during an interview for this book. They never talked again after Kassab resigned as her minister a few days before the lower house impeachment vote.

His all-male, all-white Cabinet in place, Temer did not mention gender or racial equality at all in his first speech as president to a nation where more than 50 percent identify as black or mixed race. With memes and biting commentary, many Brazilians were quick to call out the homogenous Cabinet.

"Order and Progress without women or blacks as the first step," tweeted Rio de Janeiro writer and professor André Trigueiro, playing on the phrase, "Order and Progress," that appears on the Brazilian flag. Trigueiro was also a host of GloboNews, part of the country's biggest media conglomerate, which had used its main newspaper to say Rousseff's impeachment was a way out of Brazil's crisis.[105]

"The Temer government begins with a lot of testosterone and little pigment," Trigueiro added.

In the media coverage that day, many stories made a parallel between an article about Temer's wife, Marcela, in *Veja* magazine, and the kind of Brazil the new president wanted to put forward.

The piece, titled "Beautiful, maidenlike and of the home," quoted family and friends of the former beauty pageant contestant, nearly 43 years Temer's junior, describing a daily life that harkened back to a different time in terms of gender roles, and a life that only the super-rich could afford. Marcela, who only ever worked briefly as a receptionist, reportedly spent her days taking care of the couple's 7-year-old son Michelzinho, frequenting the gym and beauty salons, and looking forward to dinners out with her husband.

"I intended this ceremony to be extremely sober and discreet, as the moment we live suggests" it should be, Temer began his speech. "However, I see the enthusiasm of our fellow lawmakers, of the governors, and I have absolute conviction that such enthusiasm derives precisely from the long coexistence we have had over time."

---

105. A pro-impeachment editorial by *O Globo* newspaper was published March 19, 2016.

Several lawmakers had jammed into the palace, including many conservatives who had not been welcome during the 13 years of Workers' Party administrations. There were no supporters outside.

"My first word to the Brazilian people is confidence," Temer said. "Confidence in the values that form the character of our people, the vitality of our democracy; confidence in the recovery of the national economy, in the potential of our country, in its social and political institutions and in the capability that, united, we shall face the challenges of this moment of great difficulty."

The inaugural address featured some bizarre moments. At one point, several photographers rushed out of the packed event to capture police using pepper spray on a small group of pro-Rousseff demonstrators outside the palace.

But there weren't any big protests in major cities. The change-of-power decision was expected, and Brazilians were clearly fatigued by a process that had taken center stage for months. For many others, who trust their own efforts more than those of any politician, it didn't really matter who was president.

About halfway through the speech, Temer lost his voice. Instead of stopping, however, he tried to power through, his face turning red and his raspy voice turning his words into a series of croaks. An aide gave him some lozenges, which appeared to help.

"It is urgent to pacify the nation and unite Brazil. It is urgent that we make an administration of national salvation. Political parties, leaders, organized entities and the Brazilian people shall collaborate to take the country out of this serious crisis that we are in," he said. "Dialogue is the first step to face the challenges to advance and assure there is growth again."

Temer also spoke briefly about the Car Wash corruption probe, which many Brazilians worried he would immediately look to quash; Many detractors argued all along that the impetus for ousting Rousseff was to put in a president who would use the levers of power to derail the investigation.

Promising to leave it alone, he called it a "reference," adding: "And as such it deserves to be followed closely and protected against any interference that could weaken it."

That promise was hard to believe given that a solid third of Temer's new Cabinet members were being investigated in the probe or had been cited in plea bargain testimony of convicts. All could claim, as was usual among Brazilian politicians in trouble, that they were innocent because they had not been convicted. But the long list of accusations made it impossible to argue that this group was prepared to clean out the rot in government:

— The new planning minister, Romero Jucá, had been cited in plea bargain testimony by Paulo Roberto Costa, the former Petrobras executive whose testimony had broken the case wide open. In March 2015, more than a year before taking his new government post, the Supreme Federal Tribunal had authorized an investigation into Jucá, then a sitting senator.
— Geddel Vieira Lima, the government secretary, was suspected of having negotiated bribes with construction company OAS.
— Henrique Eduardo Alves, the tourism minister, had had his apartment searched by federal police. He was being investigated for receiving bribes from Léo Pinheiro, president of OAS, in exchange for legislative favors.
— Bruno Araújo, minister of cities, Ricardo Barros, health minister, Raul Jungmann, defense minister, and Mendonça Filho, education and cultural minister, were on a list of "donations" made by constructor Odebrecht, seized in a major raid.

At one point in his speech, Temer declared his "absolute institutional respect to Madam President Dilma Rousseff," impersonal words about his former boss that only underscored how far apart they were.

"I do not discuss here the reasons why she was suspended. I want to stress the importance of respecting institutions and adherence to solemnity in matters of institutional issues," he said. "That is something we have to reinstate in our country. A certain ceremony that is not personal, an institutional ceremony, a ceremony in which words do not propagate bad feelings among Brazilians, but, on the contrary, propagate peace, harmony, moderation and balance among all."

Given the increasing polarization of Brazilians, perhaps these words were intended to sooth what Temer called "bad feelings" and usher in a little peace and harmony. Unfortunately, what would come next was anything but a pacifying force.

CHAPTER 18

'Stop the Bleeding'

Many Brazilians, even those who opposed impeachment and supported Rousseff, hoped that at the very least Temer's administration could put an end to the political turbulence that had rocked the country and exacerbated an already struggling economy. The first signs were not encouraging.

Several scandals began almost immediately. The once under-the-radar Temer quickly faced the equivalent of a 3 a.m. hotel fire that brought an abrupt end to the honeymoon — and dashed any hopes of reconciliation and healing.

'Stop the Bleeding'

Eleven days after Temer took office, on May 23, a bombshell story in daily newspaper *Folha de S.Paulo* seemed to confirm every suspicion of Rousseff's supporters.

"In recorded conversations, Jucá talks about a pact to stop the advance of Car Wash," read the headline.

Romero Jucá was Temer's planning minister and a longtime politician and power player in Brasília.

Folha de S.Paulo began with a published transcript of a conversation between Jucá and Sergio Machado, a former senator who had headed another state oil company, Transpetro. A few hours later, the paper released the recordings on its website.

The conversations took place in March, a few weeks before the Chamber of Deputies voted on impeachment. According to press reports, Machado, accused of corruption, had been negotiating a plea deal with Car Wash prosecutors. The implication was clear: Machado had secretly recorded the conversation with Jucá.

"We have to solve this shit. We have to change the government to stop the bleeding," Jucá said on the recording, his words spelled out in the transcripts.

After some back and forth, Machado said: "The easiest solution is to put Michel in." Jucá agreed.

Soon after the transcripts came out, Jucá called a news conference and said his comments had been taken out of context. He said he was not pushing to impeach Rousseff, but rather noting that things would be different under a new administration.

Jucá said he used the word "bleeding" to refer to Brazil's economy, which at the time was expected to contract nearly 4 percent in 2016 after an equally dismal 2015. Jucá never explained how he could have been talking about the economy when the economy was never mentioned in the conversations with Machado.

Instead, the two talked about other politicians who were being investigated in Car Wash, about keeping cases out of the hands of judge Sergio Moro and about what a Temer administration could do.

"Michel forms a government of national unity, makes a big pact, protects Lula, protects everybody," Machado said. "The country returns to normal. Nobody can take it anymore."

At his news conference, Jucá insisted he would not resign. A few hours later, he said he would take a leave of absence.

It was the second time Jucá was forced out of a cabinet position. In 2005, during the Lula administration, he left the job of pension minister after less than three months because of a series of corruption allegations. That didn't stop him from later getting reelected and keeping his influence in Brasília as a backdoor dealmaker.

Rousseff quickly weighed in, telling *Folha de S.Paulo* the day the transcripts and recordings came out, "The dialogues show that the real cause for my impeachment was an attempt to obstruct the 'Car Wash' operation. It was all made by those who thought that, without changing the government, the bleeding (of politicians) would continue."

That scandal was just the first of several to result from the recordings.

It was not the most ironic. A week later, Temer's anti-corruption czar Fabiano Silveira left as the head of the Ministry of Transparency, Inspection and Control after he was heard in the leaked audios instructing Senate President Renan Calheiros not to voluntarily give his version about a Car Wash-related investigation into alleged campaign finance violations.

"They (authorities) are going to want to go over details of what you present," Silveira is heard saying.[106]

The audio spurred an immediate reaction in the ministry. Workers there staged a protest, singing the national anthem and then mopping with soap and water on the sidewalk outside, the halls inside and even

---

106. The Silveira audio was published by news portal *G1* on May 30, 2016.

the minister's door (he was not there at the time).

Rousseff allies in Congress jumped on the development, as did Transparency International, a movement of independent chapters around the world organized to fight corruption.

"It is disappointing that the ministry in charge of transparency is now under suspicion as part of a coverup," said Transparency International in a statement, adding that it would no longer consult with the ministry until an investigation took place and a new head was put in.

Silveira reportedly met with Temer, but the optics made holding on impossible. In a resignation note, Silveira said he never interceded on Calheiros' behalf and was simply giving informal advice based on the presumption that Calheiros was innocent.

The next to go, on June 16, barely a month after his appointment, was Tourism Minister and former speaker Henrique Eduardo Alves. Machado's plea bargain testimony, released a day before Alves' resignation, alleged that more than $400,000 in bribes were funneled to Alves' campaign treasury between 2008 and 2014. Alves denied any wrongdoing in the case.

"I don't want to create awkwardness or any kind of difficulty for the government," Alves explained in a resignation letter.

Machado even had allegations against Temer: Machado said in 2012 Temer had asked him to channel $400,000 to his party's mayoral candidate in the São Paulo municipal elections as part of a kickback scheme.

Machado said the payments were legal campaign contributions made by construction firm Queiroz Galvão from Petrobras kickbacks. According to testimony by prosecutors in the plea bargain document, Temer wanted Machado "to ask for illegal funds from companies that had business with Transpetro in the form of official donations" for the campaign of Gabriel Chalita.

Temer denied any wrongdoing, calling the accusations "irresponsible" and "ludicrous."

Instead of civility and a return to governing, Temer was bringing chaos, so much so that senators who voted to impeach Rousseff were having second thoughts ahead of the final trial to decide on whether to permanently remove her.

"This is very serious," Sen. Cristovam Buarque, who voted to impeach and suspend Rousseff, told The Associated Press when reflecting on the deluge of scandals rocking Temer's fledgling administration. "We have to be even more cautious with any decision we make about Dilma's impeachment. A lot can happen before this is over."

Sen. Acir Gurgacz, who also voted for impeachment, was another of at least a half-dozen senators who publicly said they were rethinking their vote.

"The crises in the Temer government will influence my opinion, and that of the majority," Gurgacz told *Folha de S.Paulo*, adding that if the missteps continued "the scorecard can flip-flop."

It wouldn't take much to flip. The Senate vote to impeach and suspend Rousseff was 55-22, just one more than the minimum needed for permanent ouster.

It wasn't just the leaked audios that were hurting Temer.

His decision to combine some ministries, ostensibly to show the business community that he was serious about cutting fat in government, largely backfired.

When he folded the Ministry of Culture into the Ministry of Education, it set off a wave of nationwide protests, eventually pushing Temer to relent and bring back the Ministry of Culture. For many, the fact that he thought such a move would be acceptable in a country in which culture is such a deep part of the national identity — from music to celebrations like Carnival to the martial art capoeira and all the contributions of descendants of slaves, indigenous tribes and myriad immigrant groups — underscored a total tone deafness.

'Stop the Bleeding'

In protest, Grammy award winning singer Caetano Veloso sang at an occupation at the culture ministry building in Rio de Janeiro. Thousands of young Brazilians, mostly upset with the abrupt end of left-leaning administrations, showed up.

"I hate you . . . ," Veloso started singing to boisterous applause.

Then he stopped playing his acoustic guitar for the crowd to chant the president's name out loud. "Temer! Temer!"

CHAPTER 19

Under the Olympic Microscope

When Rio de Janeiro won the honor of hosting the 2016 Olympic Games, the first country in South America to do so, there were so many things that Cariocas, as local residents are called, looked forward to showcasing in their city, one of the world's most beautiful.

Visitors would take in its renowned beaches surrounded by lush green mountains. They would explore Portuguese colonial buildings downtown and colorful neighborhoods dotting the hills, such as Santa Teresa.

As they walked around, sweat on their brow from the humidity but cooled by a gentle ocean breeze, they would hear beats ooze out of apartments and restaurants, music ranging from classics like "The Girl From Ipanema" to the latest from pop star Anitta, such as "That Chick Is Crazy." In plazas and on beaches, they would feel the thump of impromptu drum circles and see groups of barefoot men and women bouncing around while doing capoeira, a martial art with movements both graceful and powerful.

Those visitors would sip on caipirinhas, made of cachaça liquor, sugar and lime, eat meats prepared in distinctive ways on a grill, along with balls of cheese bread and feijoada, a stew made of beans, beef and pork.

And, of course, crowning one peak, the enormous statue of Christ the Redeemer, one of the Seven Wonders of the Modern World, would be visible from just about anywhere in the city, a beacon of hope for the faithful that gleams under floodlights at night.

What's more, August, the last month of winter in the Southern Hemisphere, is a popular time to visit because average temperatures are in the mid-70s Fahrenheit (24 Celsius), making ocean breezes feel tropical but not oppressively hot like during the summer months of December to February.

But in the leadup to the Games, even the hopeful anticipation was often upstaged by several major problems. And these went beyond the still-looming impeachment drama that had been going all year.

— The Zika virus, which causes severe defects in fetuses, had spread from the Northeast to other parts of Brazil, including Rio. Some international health authorities even suggested that the Games be cancelled to slow its spread.
— Officials had failed to make good own pledges to clean up the water in the perennially filthy Guanabara Bay and other beaches around

the city, where many athletes would be competing in rowing, sailing, canoeing and open-water swimming events. A year-long investigation by The Associated Press had found dangerously high levels of myriad viruses in the water, which would have led to beach closures in many countries. There were daily stories about athletes getting ready to compete in the bay complaining about the filth, getting sick or taking measures like bleaching oars or rinsing their mouths after practice.

— There were constant questions about whether the venues and associated infrastructure projects would be ready on time. In April, a portion of a scenic seaside bike path built ahead of the Games collapsed after being struck by a wave, killing two people. For many Brazilians and Olympic experts, the tragedy confirmed long-held fears about shoddy and rushed construction. It also didn't help that a major addition to the metro, connecting Rio and the Olympic area in Barra da Tijuca, was badly behind schedule.

— In the first half of 2016, violence was spiking in Rio, where many favelas are controlled by drug traffickers and paramilitary groups called militias.[107]

Pacification Police Units, known by the Portuguese acronym UPP, had been created in 2008 to try to change some of the dynamics that led to constant violence. Police set up community stations in at-risk areas, increased patrols in areas run by gangs, removed weapons and worked to integrate access to public services such as utilities and garbage collection. While celebrated for lowering violence during the initial years, which helped Brazil win its Olympic bid, the program was crumbling by 2016 amid a punishing recession.

The Olympics had put a spotlight on all of this, often leading to justified

---

107. Among other foreign and local news organizations, the AP reported on this spike, which included murders.

concerns, and some exaggerated fears, that the thousands of tourists expected to descend on Rio, whom locals hoped would be charmed by the city, could instead be put at risk.

The solution that authorities came up with was to put thousands of soldiers in the streets, turning Brazil's signature city into a militarized zone. Despite the 1964-1985 military dictatorship, the armed forces were still the institution most respected by average Brazilians, according to numerous polls over the years.

Along with nonstop stories on all of these problems, there was the awkwardness of having two heads of state, one suspended and the other an interim. This, of course, also got a lot of press.

Would Rousseff, now suspended, attend the opening ceremony or any of the competitions? The Olympic Committee had invited both Rousseff and Temer. Would the two leaders, clearly enemies at this point, stand next to each other?

In an interview with GloboNews in late June, Temer said having both leaders at the opening ceremony would be awkward. He also said he hoped that Rousseff's trial would be finished before the Games began. However, that wasn't realistic. The most optimistic predictions put the vote in mid-August — which would be right in the middle of the Games.

At one point, an aide to the interim president said Rousseff would be welcome to attend the opening ceremony, but not at Temer's side in the VIP balcony. Instead, she would have to be in the stands below him.[108]

By late July, Rousseff put an end to the drama by saying she would steer clear of the ceremony and competitions. She would not attend in a "secondary position," she said during an interview with Radio France Internationale.

So, while Temer won the Olympic spotlight, it could hardly be called a coveted prize.

---

108. The comment was made to news agency Reuters on July 26, 2016.

The impeachment drama, along with the many other problems, had clearly seeped into the Olympics. For all those reasons, a majority of Brazilians were no longer excited about hosting the biggest sporting event on earth. A Datafolha poll just weeks before the kickoff laid bare the apathy: 50 percent were against hosting the Games compared to 40 percent in favor, and a whopping 63 percent felt the event would bring more damage than benefits to Brazil.[109]

While many saw Temer as generally tone-deaf, he was self-aware enough to know that, even if he didn't have to share the Olympic spotlight with his former boss, it wouldn't change how most Brazilians saw him. Polls put his approval ratings in the low teens, and he was frequently booed in public. During interviews in the days before the opening ceremony, he even joked that he was "ready" to be jeered.

In the end, Temer's role in declaring the opening of the Games on Aug. 5, 2016, was kept to a minimum. With 60,000 packed into the historic Maracanã Stadium for the opening night ceremony, Temer stepped to the podium and in less than 10 seconds fulfilled the customary head-of-state role.

Thomas Bach, the president of the International Olympic Committee, didn't even mention the name of the acting president of the host country. Neither did the announcer introducing Temer, instead simply saying "the games will be declared open."

That's when Temer spoke a single sentence. "After this marvelous spectacle, I declare the Olympic Games of Rio de Janeiro are open," the beleaguered interim president said. Some applause and many boos followed before the noise was drowned out by fireworks.

For all the drama and hand-wringing leading up the Olympics, for the most part the Games went smoothly. While the initial days saw many

---

109. The Datafolha poll was conducted and published in July 2016.

open seats at events, by the end the stands were packed. The biggest non-sports drama involved U.S. swimmer Ryan Lochte, who lied about being robbed after he and some teammates were involved in an early-morning drunken encounter. And Brazilians had some sports feats to cheer about, as its country's Olympic team finished 13th in medals, ahead of power-houses like Spain, Cuba and Canada.

The most celebrated Brazilian medal was its men's soccer gold. An Olympics was the last major tournament victory that had eluded the five-time World Cup champions. And the triumph meant more than simply Olympic glory for the troubled nation.

There was a sense of relief when a young Brazilian team led by superstar Neymar beat Germany's Olympic team in a thrilling penalty shootout at a raucous Maracanã Stadium with almost 80,000 fans. Two years earlier, during the World Cup semifinal, Germany's team thrashed Brazil 7-1.

Some hoped that the turnaround on the pitch meant things were back on track. And short of that, at least the Games were a welcome distraction for many weary Brazilians.

"At last, a bolt of gold," said the front page headline the next day on *O Globo*, one of Brazil's main dailies, with a picture of Neymar mimicking champion sprinter Usain Bolt's famous celebration. The triumphant image covered three-fourths of the page.

Through the competitions, Temer had largely stayed out of sight. A week before the closing ceremony on Aug. 21, his office said he would not be attending. No reason was given, though aides had argued that it was the mayor, not necessarily the president, who had a central role in the closing ceremony, as he would symbolically transfer the hosting duties to the leader of Japan, where the Games would be held next.[110]

---

110. News portal *G1* reported on Aug. 15, 2016, on the discussions with aides about the role of the mayor in a closing ceremony.

The decision reportedly caused consternation with Japan's organizing committee, which expected a full bilateral meeting between Temer and Japanese Prime Minister Shinzo Abe, who was traveling to Brazil for the closing ceremony. Instead, Temer sent Abe a letter, released by his office, that said he was confident the two "could meet soon."

No official reason was given for Temer's absence. There was no need. The answer was obvious.

"Brazilian Interim President Michel Temer did not attend (the closing) after he was loudly booed at the opening ceremony," read the last sentence of a Games recap article by the English-language *Japan Times*.[111]

---

111. The *Japan Times* article was published Aug. 22, 2016.

CHAPTER 20

Democracy 'On The Defendant's Bench'

The flame still flickered in the Olympic cauldron when Brazilians were asked to turn their attention from the games back to the political upheaval in Brasília.

With the opening of Dilma Rousseff's final Senate impeachment trial still more than a week away, the suspended president tried a last-minute move to change the political equation: She suggested a plebiscite allowing Brazilians to decide whether to call new elections.

In a four-page letter, which she read on television, she laid out her defense. Budget maneuvers she used were not a crime, she repeated, not now and not when her predecessors used them. Perhaps most significantly, she acknowledged making mistakes. Rousseff and the Workers' Party were not known for self-criticism, which wasn't so different from other parties.

"Errors were made, and measures and policies were not adopted," she said. "I take those criticisms with humility and determination so that we can construct a new path."

But her proposal came on Aug. 17, when Brazilians were focused on the remaining days of the Olympics. Few seemed interested in contemplating Rousseff's remaining in power on the promise that she would call for a referendum.

"Distanced from reality" was how Sen. Cássio Cunha Lima from PSDB dismissed Rousseff and her gambit. Rousseff ally Fátima Bezerra of the Workers' Party had a different take, saying, "We hope the letter will echo in Congress and the Senate, given there are still senators who haven't decided on the final vote."[112]

In the end, the letter proved little more than a distraction.

Soon after the Olympic flame was extinguished, the Senate on Aug. 25 took up the trial. Making the final decision would be 81 senators. They would serve as judges — but it soon became clear they would be just senators, thinking about their political futures.

Before the final step of the impeachment trial even began, Brazilians started reading there would be two decisions. One would be whether to show the president out. The second would be whether Rousseff could keep her "political rights." These included voting, eligibility for a job at a federal university or eligibility to seek another office in the next elections. It was, as many lawmakers say, a pure Brazilian juice; even in defeat there is some conciliation with the loser if he or she respects the outcome.

---

112. Both senators spoke with *G1* on Aug. 17, 2016.

One of the men behind the deal was the president of the Senate, Renan Calheiros. He had resisted the idea of dethroning Rousseff as much as he could.

Rousseff and Calheiros developed a somewhat personal relationship over the years, with the former guerrilla frequently asking advice from the soft-toned politician who had worked closely with every president since 1989. Also, Calheiros openly disliked Temer, who he saw as a rival in their centrist party. But being a Brasília man, he understood better than most politicians where the winds were blowing. After surviving several corruption investigations and still retaining a large part of his sway among lawmakers, he knew time had run out for the woman who used to affectionately call him "Renanzinho," or "Little Renan."

On the second day of the proceedings, Calheiros surprised his colleagues by attacking the chairwoman of the Workers' Party, Gleisi Hoffmann, who had been Rousseff's former chief of staff.

From the floor of the Senate, Hoffmann had said lawmakers did not have the moral compass to put her friend on trial. Calheiros then took the microphone and said Hoffmann's accusation was inappropriate because he had helped her and her husband get rid of a corruption probe against them in the Supreme Federal Tribunal.

"That is not true!" Hoffmann shouted.

"It can't be that a senator is saying things like this," said Calheiros, who later added: "I am very sad because this session is, above all, a statement that stupidity is endless."

Another Workers' Party senator, Lindberg Farias, said Calheiros had gone "very low."

As chaos set in, Chief Justice Ricardo Lewandowski halted the session by making his first big decision since the trial began: They'd start lunch a little early to stop the bickering.

On the following day, the first defense witness was heard. Economist Luiz Gonzaga Belluzzo, who had spent much of his early career aligned with Temer's party but became a close Workers' Party aide since the Lula years, said Rousseff did the opposite of fiscal maneuvering as her second term began in 2015.

"At the moment the economy was contracting, losing revenue, the president made a contingency of more than 8.5 billion reals. There was already a contingency of 70 billion," Belluzzo said. "There was no crime, it was a mistake of economic policy."

Belluzzo had a long presentation and was prepared to answer questions when senators returned after lunch that day. But upon return, another decision was announced: Temer allies would not question Rousseff's witnesses so the trial could be sped up.

In other words, many in the camp that wanted to oust Rousseff were so confident they had the votes that the details of the allegations no longer mattered. Still, witnesses' testimony continued through the weekend.

For those witnesses, the days were long. They were sequestered in a Brasília hotel without being able to talk to each other, watch TV or use the internet. At least for them, this was indeed a trial.[113]

On Saturday, former Finance Minister Nelson Barbosa spent eight hours detailing the government's finances and Rousseff's defense. He received questions from 33 out of 81 senators, members not allied with Temer.[114]

Barbosa argued the decrees Rousseff signed didn't end up increasing spending, and budgetary law allowed the president flexibility. He said that an administration's fiscal projections could change and be adjusted during the course of a year, and that the measure of whether budget targets had been met could only be judged at the end of the year.

---

113. News portal *G1* reported on the restrictions of the witnesses on Aug. 25, 2016.

114. A rundown of testimony was posted on the Senate's website on Aug. 27, 2016.

"The making of the decrees in question follows a procedure that has been regulated in the same way for 16 years," Barbosa said.

"The impact on the public debt depends on the spending that I do," said Barbosa. "If I spend 10 reals in a year, it increases the public debt by 10 reals no matter if it comes from this year's budget or remnants of previous budgets."

Not so, argued Sen. Antônio Anastasia, a member of PSDB and close ally of Sen. Aécio Neves. According to Anastasia, designated by Senate colleagues the chamber's rapporteur of the impeachment process, the constitution and budgetary law didn't allow for opening of credit lines if they went against the established annual fiscal target. If credit was opened, it needed to be figured into the fiscal target and reported by the administration, he argued.

The other central accusation, of fiscal peddling, or having state banks issue loans that didn't initiate from the National Treasury, garnered similar differing interpretations.

Barbosa said they could not be considered "credit operations." That distinction was important because, according to proponents of impeachment, issuing loans in that manner allowed the National Treasury to later reimburse state banks and avoid interest. It all came back to the same argument: The administration had cooked the books in order to spend and shore up support.

Through it all, Barbosa argued that moves the administration had made, the actions that were the basis of the impeachment petition, had nothing to do with the nation's economic problems. Instead, he noted that commodity prices had dropped sharply, which led to reduced tax collection, and that the rising costs of gasoline and electricity fueled inflation. He also blamed "paralysis" in Congress and proposals that were not fiscally viable, the "bomb-bills," that Cunha was putting forward.

More defense witnesses would testify, but the arguments and interpretations of both sides were largely the same.

For many Brazilians who had to go on with their lives and try to improvise their way out of a long economic crisis, this final step in the drawn-out constitutional process looked nothing but procedural. They were tired of hearing about impeachment.

So, when Rousseff arrived at the Senate for her final defense on a damp Monday morning, there were few people outside to cheer for her or to express hope she'd get shown out. At this point, no one seriously contemplated the possibility she would be returned to office — not even Rousseff.

But for the former guerrilla-turned-president, a robust defense reflected her determination to fight to the end.

The suspended president was greeted in the chamber with silence from most members. Some allies clapped, but it wasn't for long. Wearing a dark suit with embroidered flowers, Rousseff was serious and calm.

She firmly shook the hand of the chief justice before she went to the podium. She had written the speech herself in the days prior with the aid of three friends: journalists Olímpio Neto and Mário Marona, who helped shape her biography, and former justice minister José Eduardo Cardozo, a staunch defender since the start.

"At almost 70 years of age, it would be now, after being a mother and a grandmother, that I would give away the principles that have always guided me?" Rousseff began with a rhetorical question.

"In this journey to defend myself from impeachment, I got closer to the people, I had the opportunity to listen to their praise, receive their love," she continued. "I also heard harsh criticism of my administration, about mistakes that were made and measures and policies that were not adopted. I welcome that criticism with humility."

Journalists were not allowed in the chambers during her speech, which was broadcast to the nation. One senator said later that tension in the air was palpable, but it was more about the seriousness of the moment than doubt about the outcome. In any case, Rousseff's 45-minute speech was not for them. Instead, it felt intended more for any supporters still listening and for her place in history.

"In the face of accusations that are driven against me in this process, I can't help but feel, in my mouth, once again, the rough and bitter taste of injustice and arbitrary will. And thus, like in the past, I resist," she said. "Nowadays democratic rupture takes place by moral violence and constitutional pretexts so there is an appearance of legitimacy to the administration that takes over without the support of the ballot."

That didn't mean Rousseff believed those two different moments of Brazil's history were equal. On the contrary. She often said senators were in a better position to judge her than those who sentenced her to prison during military rule. Still, she believed their decision would be based on a campaign against her and her party.

"They said the elections had been fraudulent, they ordered an investigation of voting booths, invalidated my electoral accounting and after my inauguration they relentlessly sought any facts that could rhetorically justify an impeachment process," Rousseff said.

As the speech went on, Rousseff was sounding less like a member of a party and more like a tragic historic figure on the verge of damnation. A damnation that was not only hers, she warned.

"To permanently nullify my mandate is to submit me to a penalty of political death. This is the second trial I go through, and democracy has a seat, next to me, on the defendant's bench," she said, without altering her tone.

"From that time, beyond the hurtful marks of torture, there is the register in a picture of my presence in front of my executioners. At a moment I was looking at them with my head up high, while they hid their faces, fearing they would be recognized and judged by history. Today, four decades on, there is no illegal prison, no torture, my judges got here with the same popular vote that took me to the presidency. I have the utmost respect for all, but I keep my head up high, looking in the eyes of my judges."

"I suffer again with the feeling of injustice and the fear that, once more, democracy is convicted with me," she said.

Rousseff continued, her voice defiant even as senators, many looking bored, were starting to stand up or walk to the snack bar in the back of the chamber to order food and coffee.

Only a ripple of applause followed the close of her speech.

All senators surely knew by now how they would vote, but that didn't mean they were all sure it was the right decision. The winds were blowing in Temer's direction, and there was little love for the suspended president in that chamber. But the fear of making a decision that would come back to haunt them was surely on the minds of many senators. The 2018 elections, which many believed would involve a matchup between Lula and Bolsonaro, were more than two years away.

Even though it was clear that her moment had already taken place, Rousseff then answered their questions before leaving with a cold handshake from Calheiros. "Renanzinho" only months before, he was now an opponent ready to send her to the political guillotine.

Despite Rousseff's defiance throughout the trial, a conciliatory mood was captured in comments from some of her most ardent opponents.

The day after Rousseff spoke, Janaína Paschoal, a criminal lawyer and law professor in São Paulo who had been one of the principal authors of the impeachment legislation against the president, spoke on the chamber floor. Paschoal had become an internet sensation of sorts in early 2016 when she made an impassioned speech about impeachment that included shouts and wild hand waving. Testifying during Rousseff's final trial on Aug. 30, however, she was much more restrained.

"I ask for forgiveness from the president of the republic" for the pain she suffered through the process, said Paschoal, pausing and breathing so as not to cry. "I ask that she, one day, understand that I did this also thinking about the future of her grandchildren." Rousseff did not respond.

Closing arguments for and against removal were similar to what they had been in the Chamber of Deputies and the first Senate vote. But this time the atmosphere was more somber.

Neves, who began supporting the impeachment campaign shortly after losing his presidential bid in 2014, said his vote was "not to condemn a political party," adding that he respected Rousseff's biography.

"But to violate budget laws is not allowed because that is a violation of the constitution," he said.

The opposition, the press and government watchdogs were not responsible for Rousseff's mismanagement, Neves said, adding that the consequences of her illegal actions were the loss of credibility, an economic crisis and millions out of work.

"Nothing will be bigger than the truth. Absolutely nothing will speak higher than the records that we are judging here today," he said. "What will remain after this episode is a stronger country, with hope, that is once again believing in its future," he said. Rousseff didn't react to Neves' speech.

Questions by Sen. José Aníbal, and the way he asked them, did shake Rousseff. The two had known each other for 50 years, going back to their days as urban guerrillas fighting the military dictatorship. Friends say Rousseff treated Aníbal like a brother, having him over for lunch at her house when they were teenagers and dinner at the presidential palace during her first term. All that even though they ended up affiliating with competing parties: she with the leftist Workers Party and he with the right-leaning Brazilian Social Democratic Party, the same party as Neves. They also had different perspectives on their time as guerrillas; while Rousseff felt proud of her resistance, Aníbal later concluded the armed fight was a mistake.

Ahead of the Senate trial, José Eduardo Cardozo, solicitor general and top legal advisor, coached Rousseff on how he believed each lawmaker would treat her during the session. Aníbal, he said, may indeed be aggressive, based on speeches he gave before the vote.

"Don't be silly," she said, as recollected by Cardozo. "He would never do that to me."

Aníbal began his speech acknowledging their long acquaintance, giving the impression he would go easy on the president. Then he didn't.

"Madam President knows she doesn't have the minimum possibility of continuing to govern. During these long hours today she did not have the humility to recognize her mistakes," Aníbal said, ending hopes that his vote could be turned because of a personal bond. "We don't have any other alternative but to punish in obedience with the constitution and laws."

Aníbal went on to list a litany of complaints about how Rousseff had handled the economic crisis.

"Your administration doesn't exist anymore. Within hours, your presidency will not exist anymore. We aren't doing more here than what is allowed by the constitution and by the desire for change of most Brazilians, mobilized by the millions," he said.

As she heard her old friend become a foe, Rousseff grabbed onto a small towel on the Senate's presidency table. Her face turned red and the vibe in the chamber got tense, Cardozo said later in an interview.

"I leaned (toward her) and whispered, 'Stay calm,'" Cardozo said. "That was the one time in the whole impeachment process that I saw Dilma get really upset about something. She lost her focus for a while, but since she is very disciplined she managed to control herself and reply in a tone that was not too aggressive, but also revealing discomfort with how Aníbal had treated her."

After a few seconds of silence, Rousseff gave a somewhat bureaucratic answer. "I know perfectly well the way that you conduct yourself, sir. I hope you have a position of impartiality in this process and do not sentence me before due process," she said. "There is a deep flaw in this legal process. I never knew that a judge could expose his ruling at the time the witness is on the stand.

"I regret, Senator José Anibal," adding her own bit of formality when addressing a man she knew well, "that you do not fulfill the minimum request for due legal process, which secures me the right to defend myself. And I am shocked that it comes from you, who has known me for many years."

Chief-Justice Lewandowski, noticing Rousseff's emotions were running high despite her calm words, offered a break. The president refused and asked for the next senator to start his line of inquiry.

"It was lamentable. Nobody can deny their own history," Rousseff later said of Aníbal's speech, adding that she never wanted to speak with him again.

There was also some disappointment with the vote of Sen. Cristovam Buarque, who was once a well-known member of the Workers' Party and a former education minister under Lula. He had moved to the center many years before, but reports of talks he had with Rousseff before the trial suggested he could vote with her.

"I want to help recover progressive forces. We are impeaching not only Dilma, but also an old left," he said from the podium.

Few senators who were not members of the Workers' Party took the stand to defend her.

Sen. Roberto Requião was seen as a rogue member of Temer's party. With longstanding leftist views, he claimed to represent the original wing of PMDB. He was in a clear minority during the trial, promising to vote against impeachment from the start.

If the Senate "sentences the president even without guilt, I hope that everyone is aware of what could come," he said. "It will not be the first time that vultures will fall onto our land."

Requião ended his speech with a threat: "Are you ready for civil war?" Some colleagues laughed. Many weren't even listening.

Perhaps the only speech many Brazilians were keen to listen to was of former President Fernando Collor de Mello, now a senator. After all, he had been impeached in 1992 amid a web of corruption that had been denounced by his own brother. Rousseff and Collor had had a good relationship over the years, with the senator openly showing his appreciation for Rousseff in what was seen as a sort of rehabilitation for him on the national stage.

"Impeachment is a constitutional, urgent remedy in the presidential system when the government commits crimes of responsibility and loses control of the economic and political reins of the country," he said, arguing his own situation was totally different because he had been scammed.

Collor was removed from office after a broad coalition of leftists, conservatives and liberals agreed he had tainted the presidency with scandals. He was impeached by the lower house and resigned shortly before the vote in the Senate. But senators didn't care, voting to remove him from office anyway and suspend his political rights for eight years.

Collor left Brazil for Miami, where he lived in disgrace until he had his political rights restored. In 2006, he was elected senator for his home state of Alagoas, managing to slowly return to the public eye.

Fast-forward to 2016. "Now the suspended administration transformed its management into a foretold tragedy," said Collor, adding: "She committed a crime."

When the speeches were finally finished, only one formality remained for Rousseff's judges: the rendering of their verdict.

CHAPTER 21

Tristeza

"Senators, you may vote," said Chief Justice Ricardo Lewandowski.

The arguments, both for and against impeachment and removal, had been made repeatedly for a year. The protests, both for and against, had taken place all over the country. The backroom negotiations, both to try to keep Dilma Rousseff in office and oust her once and for all, had all happened.

At this point, voting was all that was left. And it didn't take long.

In less than 3 minutes, all 81 senators cast their votes electronically. On a large board above the chamber, the name of each appeared as they voted, though the tally did not show up until all had made their decision.

It was around 3:35 p.m. on Aug. 31, 2016, when Lewandowski proclaimed the final result: 61 voted to remove Rousseff and 20 were opposed.

Some shouts of celebration and some boos could be heard, but even combined, they were more white noise than a loud roar.

Many senators were simply relieved that it was finally over.

Rousseff, now the former president, did not hold back her own reaction. She took to social media, arguing on Twitter that impeachment was akin to throwing "54 million Brazilian votes in the garbage."

"The coup is against the people and the nation. It's misogynist. It's homophobic. It's racist. It's the imposition of intolerance, prejudice and violence," she said in another tweet.

But there was still one more decision to be made: whether Rousseff would also be stripped of her political rights for eight years. If convicted in the final trial phase, the penalty was removal from the presidency and a prohibition from holding office for eight years.

When President Fernando Collor de Mello was impeached in 1992, there was no consideration of letting him retain his political rights; over the following eight years, he tried unsuccessfully to get the prohibition overturned in the courts.

For Rousseff, however, the Senate made the question of political rights a separate vote. And on this vote, about 30 minutes after the first, Rousseff prevailed. Although voting 42-36 against her, the Senate fell short of the 54 senators needed, or two-thirds of the chamber.

It was a minor victory for Rousseff, albeit an arguably bizarre and logically strained one. If the president had committed crimes so grave that she deserved to be removed from office, shouldn't she also be barred from seeking other political posts? Or even jailed?

For many Brazilians, particularly supporters of the Workers' Party, the fact that the only consequence for her "crimes of responsibility" was that she lost her current job underscored that all along the only goal was removal.

Even Rousseff herself found no consolation in the win. "It was a mockery," she said during an interview. "It really doesn't have an explanation."

The list of people who wanted Rousseff gone was a long one, ranging from politicians on the right and those being investigated in the Car Wash probe to many average Brazilians who were exhausted from the paralysis and in many cases suffering the economic consequences of the recession. In that sense, Rousseff had become a burden too heavy for the political system to keep carrying.

Not long after the two votes, Rousseff held a press conference at the presidential residence, her bunker since she had been suspended from office. It would be her final appearance before a small crowd there. She had to leave within a few days.

Wearing a red suit and surrounded by members of the Workers' Party, Rousseff said senators had decided to "tear up the constitution." Her ouster would go down as one of "the great injustices of history."

Politicians accused of corruption were clearly hoping that the "coup" would help them survive, she said, adding that removing a democratically elected leader, the first female president in Brazil's history, was an affront to voters, social movements and the millions who had moved out of poverty during the Workers' Party's 13 years in power.

"This is a fraud that we will fight in all ways possible," she said, though outside the palace there was little sign of unrest or interest in a continued fight.

Temer, who had officially become president for the rest of the term, through 2018, spoke to the nation via a recorded video that evening.

"The uncertainty is over," he proclaimed.

Temer promised to jump-start the economy by attracting foreign investment, getting unemployed Brazilians back to work and restoring confidence in governing.

"We comfort ourselves in knowing that the worst is over," he said, words that were not comforting for a populace that had already witnessed several scandals during his interim administration.

Nonetheless, for all the fights and conflicting political narratives surrounding impeachment, a somewhat peaceful transfer of power had happened. Rousseff, for all her faults, had been a democrat through it all. She never put the army on the streets, as some supporters had suggested. And even some of her staunchest adversaries recognized she did not use her office to derail a process that was clearly building momentum against her at each stage.

Her experience during the dictatorship helped her keep perspective about how history may judge her.

"During impeachment, I was the only democrat," Rousseff reflected during an interview in 2021.

"I was 16 when the dictatorship began and during that time, and historically, each time there was a kind of conquest it hurt the development of the country," she said. "I believed we could lose that war there (impeachment) but not the final battle for democracy."

Rousseff's top lawyer and ally, José Eduardo Cardozo, also said their fight was ultimately about setting the record straight, adding that it was clear to him she would likely be removed after the Chamber of Deputies commission vote in April 2016.

"We thought it was worth mounting a defense. For people outside Brazil and for history, we wanted to show she was innocent," said Cardozo during an interview.

In any case, Rousseff's low popularity didn't offer her much of a base. Some of the hardcore members of the Workers' Party were already thinking about the 2018 elections and hoped to bring Lula back to power, though he was increasingly facing the risk of jail time. For many of those, Rousseff was a nuisance.

For many in Brazil, a country that has always aspired to great things, the proceedings were a reality check. It was as if Brazilians were seeing their country in the mirror: deep divisions, a vulnerable democracy, a fragile economy and a political class that on the left, center and right looked more like fixtures of a banana republic than serious statesmen.

For supporters of the Workers' Party and many progressives, Rousseff's ousting was a form of déjà vu. It was akin to watching a film from 1964, only instead of the military intervening with force, it was the upper classes using questionable claims of presidential crimes to oust a fatally weakened leader.

For detractors of the Workers Party and opponents of Rousseff that cut across the political spectrum, the ends clearly justified the means. In their minds, Rousseff was a bad president who had become too unpopular to stay on and simply deserved to go. Indeed, the argument that she simply couldn't continue was a central reason that many in Congress gave to remove her.

The overall situation in Brazil, however, raised questions about whether removing her would solve anything or actually exacerbate the problems. No matter who was in office, it would take years for Brazil's economy to recover. The corruption scandal and political problems didn't help, but at the heart of the crisis were historically low commodity prices, which no politician had control over.

The Car Wash investigation, which had in its crosshairs many members of Congress and Temer's Cabinet, was going to go on for the foreseeable future. In fact, if Temer's interim government was any measure, middle-of-the-night raids and high-profile arrests would surely continue.

And the solutions being put forward by politicians on the hard-right wanting to fill the void, such as Congressman Jair Bolsonaro, were simple at best and at worst could be detrimental. Harkening back to the supposedly simpler time of the military dictatorship, demonizing left-leaning policies and touting "family values" wasn't going to solve the economic crisis, rid the country of entrenched corruption or address widespread inequality that fuels many of Brazil's long-standing problems.

On the other hand, with Rousseff so weakened, could the country really hang on another 2½ years until her term ended? Prolonged paralysis in Congress could have wide-ranging implications, from budgets to national security.

At the heart of democracy is winning free and fair elections, and Rousseff had clearly done that. But once in office, leaders are expected to lead and solve problems, no matter what situations come their way. While many enemies were clearly trying to make Rousseff fail, she herself was failing as a leader. In that sense, could her continuation in office really be justified?

History will judge who was right and who was wrong.

A week after her official removal, Rousseff discreetly left Brasília for Porto Alegre, her adopted home after her early years fighting the military dictatorship.

Her modest apartment is located behind a supermarket on the same Avenida Copacabana where she lived for two decades in a house with her ex-husband Carlos Araújo, on the shores of the Guaíba River (Araújo died in August 2017, a year after Rousseff was removed).

The neighborhood, where she spent most of her adult life, is called Tristeza. In English, the name means sadness. But rather than sad, her assessment of life now is reflective, at times wistful, even hopeful.

"I came back because I wanted back a bit of my life before becoming president," Rousseff said in an interview at her home library a year and a half after her removal.

"I came to ride my bike near the river, see my two grandchildren and breathe outside that toxic environment that Brasília has now. I want to be near people who suffered with me, not only during this coup, but throughout the years," she said.

"I came back because from here I can dream again that Brazil will be better in the future."

Since returning to Porto Alegre, she says she continues to wake up at 5:30 a.m. to go cycling, just as she did in Brasília, even in her worst moments in the country's top job.

Now there are no journalists or supporters following her around. At best, she sometimes has a friend joining her. Her usual company is two agents from Brazil's Institutional Security Cabinet. They follow her closely for safety in a still divided Brazil. Thanks to the office she was thrown out of, she'll have that modest protection for the rest of her life.

Epilogue

In the years after Dilma Rousseff was ousted, there were predictable outcomes and some surprises. Unfortunately, many had this in common: They deepened divisions in Brazil.

While Rousseff has not been charged with a crime, many of the major players in the drama, including those who were behind her ouster, have gone to jail or at the very least have been widely discredited. And her downfall helped shift the government in Latin America's most populous nation far to the right — what many see as an echo of a new kind of authoritarianism in several countries around the world.

In May 2016, just weeks after Eduardo Cunha successfully guided the impeachment legislation through the Chamber of Deputies, the Supreme Federal Tribunal Justice Teori Zavascki removed him from office as various corruption investigations gained traction. He was later arrested.

Not only was Cunha allowed by both his fellow members of Congress and the country's top court to guide the impeachment legislation before being forced to answer for criminal allegations, but he was allowed to do all that despite Attorney General Rodrigo Janot's request to the Supreme Federal Tribunal on Dec. 16, 2015, to remove him.

In his decision, Zavascki justified the time it took by saying the request had been submitted right before the summer recess (December-February in the Southern Hemisphere) and only "at a recent date" could the petition be fully evaluated.

José Eduardo Cardozo, Rousseff's top legal adviser, said Zavascki told him that the top court "would only put it to a vote after the impeachment process was finished, without more justification."

In January 2017, Zavascki died in a plane crash outside the coastal town of Paraty in Rio de Janeiro state.

While it is impossible to know why it took the court so long to act — there are many potential factors — had Cunha been removed sooner, the impeachment process might not have happened at all, or it might have been overseen by somebody more objective and less critical of Rousseff.

In early 2017, Cunha was convicted of corruption, tax evasion and money laundering, and Car Wash Judge Sergio Moro sentenced him to more than 15 years in prison. For supporters of Rousseff and the Workers' Party, the outcome was galling: The person who had exerted defining influence in toppling a democratically elected president was a convicted crook. (Because of coronavirus, Cunha was allowed to transition to home arrest in early 2020).

The remaining 2½ years of Rousseff's second term, during which Brazil was led by President Michel Temer, were anything but smooth. One scandal after another rocked Temer's administration, including many allegations of corruption by Temer himself. Things got so bad that in May 2017 many expected him to resign after a recording was released that purported to capture him endorsing the payment of hush money to Cunha.

"I will not resign," Temer said emphatically during a hastily arranged news conference. In it, though not denying that he had been recorded saying what he did, he denied he had ever endorsed payments.

Ever the survivor, Temer managed to stay afloat. He would survive two votes in the Chamber of Deputies that would have suspended him from office to stand trial for alleged corruption. He would also survive a vote by the country's top electoral court on whether to remove him from office due to alleged illegal campaign financing of the Rousseff-Temer ticket.

Amid so many problems, most of Temer's pro-market agenda tanked, one exception being a large reform to the labor code.

Ever the optimist, Temer even briefly toyed with running for president in the 2018 elections. That despite approval ratings in the single digits, just like Rousseff before she was ousted, and boos wherever he went.

A few months after leaving office on Jan. 1, 2019, Temer was arrested on charges that construction company Engevix paid him bribes in exchange for a contract to build a nuclear plant in the southern part of Rio de Janeiro state. Prosecutors also alleged, though this was not included in the actual charges, that Temer had been participating in pay-to-play deals since the 1980s.

Less than a week later, Temer was out of jail after a judge ruled he didn't pose a risk to the investigation and could fight the charges while free. Briefly arrested again in May 2019, Temer has continued to fight several investigations while out of jail. Despite his legal tangles, he has been given political assignments by President Jair Bolsonaro, such as leading a humanitarian mission to Lebanon in early 2020 after a massive port explosion.

With Rousseff ousted and the Workers' Party sullied from the Car Wash investigation, Lula had few friends in high enough places to help him fight investigations that got closer to him each day.

In July 2017, Lula was convicted of corruption in a complex case that accused the former president of receiving a beachfront apartment and repairs as kickbacks from construction company OAS. Moro sentenced Lula to 9 ½ years in prison.

Early the next year, the conviction was upheld and the sentence increased to just over 12 years. In April 2018 Lula was arrested — after a nail-biting stalemate between security forces and members of the union he once led. He was flown to Curitiba and began serving his sentence.

That didn't mean that Lula immediately gave up his plan to run for the presidency in October 2018, however. For months, from jail Lula insisted he planned to run, even though his conviction made him ineligible and higher courts were clearly in no rush to deal with his latest round of appeals.

While Lula dreamed of a return to power — and polls showed he would likely win — his reluctance to name a successor was also based on a stark reality: He didn't have many viable candidates from whom to choose. Many senior members of the Workers' Party were ensnared in the Car Wash investigation and others on the left were more likely to criticize the once dominant party's errors than get behind a jailed standard-bearer.

In August 2018, just two months before the election, Lula named former São Paulo Mayor Fernando Haddad as the party's candidate. An economist, lawyer and university professor, Haddad had been education minister under both Lula and Rousseff. He clearly had the resume to compete for the country's top job, but his record in elections wasn't inspiring. After winning the mayorship of Brazil's biggest city in 2012, he lost his reelection bid four years later.

Haddad also lacked charisma, national name recognition and time to introduce himself to voters in a nation geographically larger than the continental United States. What's more, he had what appeared to be an impossible mission: present himself as a clean candidate above the corruption fray while also harnessing the power of Lula, the country's most recognizable politician — now jailed for corruption.

In the runup to the 2018 elections, many analysts believed that a severely fractured left combined with a lackluster Workers' Party candidate would boost traditional center-right contender Geraldo Alckmin of the PSDB. The former governor of São Paulo had experience at that level, having reached the runoff against Lula in 2006. After the impeachment of Rousseff, he had captured the support of several parties and in subsequent years had held off internal adversaries Aécio Neves and São Paulo Mayor João Doria. In early 2018, the financial markets bet heavily on Alckmin.

But Alckmin's flat persona, his old style of compromise politics, and the PSDB's deep involvement in the impeachment proceedings and in the failing Temer administration proved to be liabilities at a time when many Brazilians, exhausted by the drama of the previous years, were looking beyond the establishment. By mid-2018, with the campaign getting to the most intense stages, polls showed that much of Alckmin's support was moving to Bolsonaro on the far right.

In the decades before running for office, Bolsonaro was seen by many Brazilians as fringe, somebody always likely to say something crazy but never capable of building a national campaign and winning the presidency. He was also seen as an intellectual lightweight with little to show in terms of policy wins, or even ideas beyond military dictatorship nostalgia, during 27 years in Congress.

A review by The Associated Press of Bolsonaro's legislative record ahead of the election found that only two bills he had submitted had become law, one to make an experimental cancer drug available and another to extend a tax credit to the information technology industry.[115] Instead of bold policy ideas, many of his legislative filings were attempts to extend benefits to police or military personnel or call for commemorations, such as one to celebrate the 50th anniversary of the beginning of the dictatorship.

Despite Bolsonaro's thin resume, the Car Wash investigation, Rousseff's ouster and a struggling economy all added to his master narrative: that Brazil had gone astray in moving left under the Workers' Party, that corruption needed to be ruthlessly stomped out and that only a return to "family values," and to more idyllic, simple times, could put the country on the right path. Bolsonaro convinced many voters that graft under the Workers' Party was a key reason the economy had tanked, and only an honest president could change that.

Still, Bolsonaro was not a good public speaker and despite his lead in

---

115. The AP investigation was published Oct. 1, 2018.

the polls, many believed Haddad or Alckmin could change the equation during national debates by exposing Bolsonaro's character flaws and a platform that amounted to simpleton solutions. For example, Bolsonaro promised to crack down on violence in part by making it easier for Brazilians to own and carry guns and to shield police from prosecution in the case they kill people during an operation.

Numerous studies around the world have shown that more guns in a society leads to more firearm violence, not less. What's more, police forces in some of Brazil's biggest cities, including Rio de Janeiro, were already some of the most lethal in the world and terrifying for many average people, particularly in poor neighborhoods. These were things that Haddad and Alckmin could point out on a national stage, and if Bolsonaro said anything racist, homophobic or sexist, as he very well might, that would help make the case that he was unfit for office.

Then something happened that likely helped Bolsonaro's chances enormously: On Sept. 6, 2018, one month before the first round of voting, he was stabbed and hospitalized in critical condition while campaigning in Juiz de Fora, a few hours drive north from Rio de Janeiro. The attacker, Adélio Bispo de Oliveira, was quickly arrested and deemed to be mentally ill.

De Oliveira had once affiliated with the leftist Socialism and Liberty Party, and this fact allowed Bolsonaro's strong propaganda machine on messaging apps to present the incident as a harbinger of the danger to average citizens if progressives returned to the presidency.

And another result of the stabbing: Bolsonaro's campaign said he couldn't show up to debates, under doctors' orders. Whether that was truly the case — many argued that he recovered enough to be able to debate — who could criticize that strategy? Limiting his exposure in uncontrolled environments, Bolsonaro was able to do the kind of campaigning he was best at, which essentially involved him hosting Facebook Lives and producing television and radio ads.

Sitting at a table in a T-shirt, sometimes alone and sometimes with one or two supporters, he presented himself as an everyman, a stern father with no-nonsense solutions for a nation that was struggling because of misbehavior. That resonated with many voters.

In the first round, Bolsonaro got 46 percent, a strong showing but just short of enough to win outright. Haddad got nearly 30 percent and Ciro Gomes, also on the center-left, got 12.5 percent. Alckmin got less than 5 percent.

In the runoff three weeks later, Bolsonaro handily beat Haddad, 55 to 45 percent. The hard-right leader's wave was so big that many members of Congress and governors came to office on his coattails. In Congress, Bolsonaro and his Social Liberal Party (he would separate from the party in 2019) proceeded to enact policies that included making it easier for civilians to own guns, rolling back environmental regulations, increasing mining in the Amazon and eliminating or defunding programs started by the Workers' Party, such as having Cuban doctors work in rural areas where it was hard to recruit Brazilian counterparts. Bolsonaro, a big fan of then U.S. President Donald Trump, also suggested pulling Brazil from the Paris accords on climate.

Bolsonaro would also persuade Moro, who for years claimed no interest in politics, to become his justice minister. For many Rousseff supporters, Moro's decision to join Bolsonaro's administration was confirmation that the judge had harbored his own political ambitions and from the beginning had been partisan in his dealings with left-wing politicians (though some politicians on the right had also been jailed). It was also a risky career move for Moro because to take the Cabinet position he had to step down as a federal judge and pass the baton of the Car Wash investigation to others.

In April 2020, Moro left the administration after Bolsonaro put in a new head of the federal police, a move Moro claimed the president did to be able to get confidential investigative reports. Two of Bolsonaro's sons, also politicians, were being investigated for corruption (Bolsonaro has always denied he tried to interfere with the federal police and insisted it was his prerogative to pick whomever he wanted).

The year 2018 was also a defining one for Rousseff, who had never stopped arguing that she was the victim of a "coup." The former president ran for a Senate seat from her home state of Minas Gerais.

"We are reaffirming democracy in Brazil, which was badly beaten during the impeachment process and what came after impeachment, advancing agendas that didn't have a single vote in the election of 2014," Rousseff told daily *Folha de S.Paulo* the morning of the Oct. 7, 2018, election.

Polls leading up to the election predicted Rousseff would win, but she ended up a distant fourth place. Voters in Minas Gerais clearly said they had no appetite to see Rousseff back on stage, even if she had been unfairly ousted a few years earlier.

While rejected at the polls, Rousseff has been vindicated in other ways.

Unlike so many others who helped bring about her downfall, to date she has not been accused of a crime.

And one of her central accusations — that Temer was part of the conspiracy to oust her — has been supported by Cunha, according to a book he wrote from jail. *Bye, Dear: A Diary of Impeachment,* came out in April 2021. Cunha wrote that Temer was "the most important and active" participant in the push to oust Rousseff and he negotiated "every job to be given to every party or congressman who would vote in favor of the opening (of impeachment debate)."

According to Cunha, everybody voting for Rousseff's ouster knew what they would get in return.

"Nothing was for free," said Cunha. "Temer sought Dilma's downfall. Temer plotted his rise."

Not surprisingly, Temer has denied Cunha's claim in various local media interviews. In October 2020, Temer released *The Choice*, a book in which he argues that he "managed to overcome a serious crisis and introduce an agenda to Brazil." Based on conversations between Temer and

Denis Rosenfield, a friend and philosophy professor, the 220-page book is thin on details of the impeachment process. Temer does, however, insist he never craved Rousseff's job and weighs in on why he believes Cunha went after the president.

"The Workers' Party attacked the speaker of the Chamber of Deputies too much, and in the face of that aggression he had no alternative," Temer wrote.

Temer also complained about an accusation he frequently still hears. "'Coup monger' . . . all the time," Temer said. "This is a political move that shows how we have little appreciation for institutionality." In other words, Temer's rise to the presidency was mandated by the constitution.

Temer declined numerous requests in 2020 and 2021 to be interviewed for this book. He, his aides, his wife and one of his daughters were reached by phone, email and Twitter. Most never responded. His publicity agent, Elsinho Mouco, made several promises of an interview at future dates but never delivered.

As of this writing, Temer has not answered many relevant questions related to impeachment. What role did he play behind the scenes? Why did he write a letter to Rousseff (that would be leaked) outlining his disagreements and not just talk to her? How does he respond to the accusation by Cunha that he whipped votes for impeachment? And does he believe, as many analysts today do, that the impeachment proceedings helped propel Bolsonaro to the presidency?

Cunha, jailed, could not be interviewed in time for this book.

Despite a clearly fraught relationship between Rousseff and Temer, Temer has expressed respect for Rousseff's character. In a rare interview about the impeachment process, given to *Veja* magazine in January 2021, Temer said Rousseff had committed a crime in the "institutional sense," the so-called "pedaladas fiscais," or "fiscal maneuvering" of moving money between budgets, but she had not committed a crime in the criminal sense.

"Sometimes the former president is accused of an eventual dishonesty," said Temer. "I coexisted (worked) with her, of course in a decorative way, but I must say she has unparalleled honesty."

These days, Rousseff has scathing things to say about the man who used to be her No. 2.

"Traditionally, traitors are weak, and Temer was weak," Rousseff said during an interview in 2021, one of several for this book.

In her mind, Temer was simply a puppet doing what he was told. "Cunha was the one moving the strings from behind," she said.

Whoever was the true shotcaller, Cunha claims responsibility for all that happened.

"Want it or not, the person responsible for all this impeachment process was me," Cunha said in his book. "Many sought to inherit that glory, but either they didn't take part in anything or were in mere supporting roles, including the authors of the request of the proceedings made to the Chamber of Deputies and accepted by me."

Time has brought clarity to how Bolsonaro benefited and positioned himself to take advantage of the chaos.

"Bolsonaro was really a maverick in the impeachment proceedings," Cunha said in his book.

Bolsonaro "was a Trojan Horse for neoliberalism and the hard-right," said Rousseff, adding her contention, one widely accepted by analysts today, that impeachment paved the way for Bolsonaro.

Time has also raised questions about the legal processes against Lula, which in 2016 added fire to the impeachment push.

In March 2021, the Supreme Federal Tribunal ruled that Moro had been biased in how he conducted Lula's corruption trial. That came after leaked messages published by *The Intercept Brasil* in 2019 showed apparent collusion between the prosecutors trying Car Wash cases and Moro when he was a federal judge ruling on those cases.

In a separate decision, the court also annulled the convictions against

Lula on the grounds that he was tried in the wrong jurisdiction — Curitiba, where Moro was based, and not the capital of Brasília. Those decisions opened the door for Lula to run for the presidency again in 2022.

Even if Rousseff appears to be done with electoral campaigns, she remains an active voice against the Bolsonaro administration and is still looked to as a figure of national stature.

She made national news in January 2021, when, during the coronavirus pandemic, she and other former presidents were invited by São Paulo Gov. João Doria to take a COVID-19 vaccine made by Chinese pharmaceutical company Sinovac. The idea of the act was to encourage Brazilians to get vaccinated.

Rousseff, a cancer survivor and well into her 70s, said she appreciated the offer but declined. Instead, she said she would wait in line with other Brazilians until it was her turn.

Aftermath

Former Chamber of Deputies Speaker Eduardo Cunha is seen being led by police in Curitiba after being arrested on Oct. 20, 2016, on corruption charges. Earlier in 2016, Cunha led the impeachment push against President Dilma Rousseff, who was permanently removed from office. (AP Photo/Denis Ferreira)

Brazilian singer Caetano Veloso performs at a protest against President Michel Temer in Rio de Janeiro on May 28, 2017. Temer was very unpopular among Brazilians on the left, in part because of controversial decisions like announcing the combining of the cultural and education ministries. (AP Photo/Leo Correa)

Protesters demanding the resignation of President Michel Temer clash with police in Brasília on May 24, 2017. Amid several scandals in 2016 and 2017, Temer's already low popularity dropped even further, prompting many protests and demands that he resign. (AP Photo/Eraldo Peres)

Former President Luiz Inácio Lula da Silva is seen being escorted by federal police in Curitiba, Brazil, on April 7, 2018. Lula began serving a sentence of 12 years and one month after being convicted of corruption. (AP Photo/Leo Correa)

Presidential hopeful Jair Bolsonaro poses for a photo with cadets during a ceremony marking Army Day in Brasília on April 18, 2018. Bolsonaro, a former Army captain, often spoke favorably about the 1964-1985 dictatorship and drew on his time with the military during the campaign. (AP Photo/Eraldo Peres)

Presidential candidate Jair Bolsonaro is carried by supporters after being stabbed while campaigning on Sept. 6, 2018, in the city Juiz de Fora. Bolsonaro was hospitalized, would undergo surgeries and ultimately survived. Happening just two months before the first round of elections, the stabbing changed the course of the campaign. (AP Photo/Fernando Goncalves)

Former President Dilma Rousseff speaks at a Workers' Party national convention in São Paulo on Aug. 4, 2018. The convention confirmed the candidacy of former President Luiz Inácio Lula da Silva for the October 2018 elections even though a corruption conviction barred him from running. (AP Photo/Nelson Antoine)

Workers' Party presidential candidate Fernando Haddad speaks during a rally in São Paulo on Sept. 13, 2018. The former São Paulo mayor was made the Workers' Party standard bearer less than two months before the election. He tried to both harness the popularity of former President Luiz Inácio Lula da Silva and, in light of Lula's corruption conviction, present himself as his own man to general voters. (AP Photo/Andre Penner)

Supporters of presidential candidate Jair Bolsonaro rally in São Paulo on Sept. 30, 2018, about a week before the first round of voting. The woman in the front is seen making her fingers in the shape of pistols, something that Bolsonaro, a former Army captain, frequently did during his 27-year career in Congress. (AP Photo/Andre Penner)

President Jair Bolsonaro waves to the crowd from the presidential palace on Jan. 1, 2019, the day he was inaugurated. To the left is Bolsonaro's wife, Michelle Bolsonaro, and to the right is outgoing President Michel Temer. (AP Photo/Silvia Izquierdo)

Former President Michel Temer is seen through a window of a federal police station in Rio de Janeiro on March 25, 2019. Temer was released from jail a week after being arrested on corruption charges. (AP Photo/Leo Correa)

Justice Minister Sergio Moro announces he is resigning during press conference in Brasília on April 24, 2020. Moro broke with President Jair Bolsonaro after the president decided to change the head of the country's federal police. (AP Photo/Eraldo Peres)

President Jair Bolsonaro, on the left, and former President Michel Temer, attend a ceremony on Aug. 12, 2020, at an air base outside São Paulo ahead of sending a planeload of supplies to Lebanon in the wake of a major explosion in Beirut. Despite corruption cases against him, Temer, whose parents emigrated to Brazil from Lebanon, was tapped to lead Brazil's efforts to help the Middle Eastern country. (AP Photo/Andre Penner)

Former President Luiz Inácio Lula da Silva speaks at the Metalworkers Union headquarters in São Bernardo do Campo, Brazil, on March 10, 2021, after a judge threw out the two convictions against him. Early polls show Lula could beat Bolsonaro in the 2022 presidential elections. (AP Photo/Andre Penner)

Acknowledgments

There are so many people we want to thank. Peter Costanzo, AP's director of programming who manages AP's book publishing division, believed in this project from the first conversations and drafts. That confidence, and his green light, helped us believe in ourselves and this book.

Editor Chris Sullivan was terrific all around — guiding rewrites, pushing for clarity and deeper reporting in several chapters and elevating the prose at every stage.

Many journalists and academics, some friends and others we didn't know before reaching out, provided valuable feedback in reading early drafts:

- Tim Padgett, Americas Editor at WLRN Public Radio & Television in Miami.
- Thomas Traumann, former Social Communication minister of Dilma Rousseff and political consultant.
- Jon Lee Anderson, staff writer at *The New Yorker*.
- Stephanie Dennison, chair of Brazilian Studies at Leeds University.
- Olímpio Cruz Neto, former press secretary for Dilma Rousseff.
- James Green, professor of modern Latin American history and Brazilian Studies at Brown University.

Special thanks to Julianna Barbassa, Latin America and Caribbean Editor at *The New York Times* and a former *Associated Press* colleague, for writing the foreword. She also provided valuable feedback and encouragement.

Finally, we want to acknowledge each other. In early 2017, just a few months after Rousseff was permanently removed, Mauricio proposed to Peter a book on the fallen leader. That initial idea evolved into this narrative.

Along the way, there were many times we could have given up, and almost did. We had plenty of good reasons, including the birth of Mauricio's daughter in 2019 and Peter's transfer from Brazil to Arizona in the same year. That we found a way to continue working on the book on top of full-time work, intense family demands and a global pandemic that turned all of our lives upside down, speak to our deep commitment to each other and to telling this story.

Key Moments of Impeachment

Dec. 2, 2015: Chamber of Deputies Speaker Eduardo Cunha puts forward legislation to impeach President Dilma Rousseff for alleged violations of fiscal laws in managing the federal budget.

Dec. 7, 2015: Vice President Michel Temer releases a letter airing beefs he has with Rousseff and signaling his rupture from the administration.

Dec. 16, 2016: Attorney General Rodrigo Janot requests that the Supreme Federal Tribunal remove Cunha from office to keep him from tampering with corruption allegations against him.

Dec. 17, 2015: Cunha's impeachment efforts face a setback when the Supreme Federal Tribunal rules against his fast-track plan to put Rousseff directly on trial in the Senate in the case that the legislation is passed in the Chamber of Deputies.

Dec. 18, 2015: Rousseff's finance minister, Joaquim Levy, resigns, underscoring the president's struggles to improve the ailing economy.

Feb. 23, 2016: Marketing expert João Santana and wife Mônica Moura, members of Rousseff's inner circle, are arrested on accusations they had received millions in illicit funds via offshore accounts controlled by construction company Odebrecht.

March 3, 2016: Media reports emerge on a leaked plea bargain by Sen. Delcídio do Amaral, a member of the Workers' Party and government whip who had been jailed since late 2015 for allegedly trying to interfere with the Car Wash investigation.

March 4, 2016: Car Wash judge Sergio Moro compels former President Luiz Inácio Lula da Silva to testify about several alleged corruption cases against him.

March 6, 2016: Marcelo Odebrecht, former CEO of construction giant, is sentenced to 19 years in prison for corruption.

March 13, 2016: Massive protests nationwide call for Rousseff's impeachment and an end to corruption.

March 16, 2016: Judge Moro releases wiretapped conversations between Lula and several others, including Rousseff.

March 17, 2016: Lula is sworn in as Rousseff's chief of staff. Before he assumes office, however, a federal judge blocks the appointment.

March 29, 2016: Temer's Brazilian Democratic Movement Party (PMDB) formally breaks from Rousseff's ruling coalition.

April 11, 2016: An audio recorded by Temer, which features him laying out his vision for the future of the country, is leaked. The same day, a Chamber of Deputies commission approves the impeachment legislation with a 38-27 vote.

April 17, 2016: The Chamber of Deputies votes 367-137 to impeach Rousseff, moving the legislation to the Senate.

May 5, 2016: Supreme Federal Tribunal Justice Teori Zavascki orders Cunha indefinitely suspended from office on allegations that he was using his position to tamper with corruption investigations.

May 12, 2016: The Senate votes 55-22 to suspend Rousseff and move the impeachment legislation to the trial phase to decide on permanent removal. Temer takes over as president.

May 23, 2016: Daily *Folha de S.Paulo* reports on recorded conversations by Romero Jucá, Temer's planning minister, allegedly discussing a plan to stop the Car Wash investigation that involved putting Temer in office.

Aug. 31, 2016: The Senate votes 61-20 to permanently remove Rousseff from office, allowing Temer to serve the rest of her term, which goes through Dec. 31, 2018.

Main Players and Political Parties

PRESIDENT DILMA ROUSSEFF: Brazil's first woman president, Rousseff was elected in 2010 and re-elected in 2014 after serving as chief of staff to President Luiz Inácio Lula da Silva. Rousseff was impeached and removed from office in a controversial process. Detractors said she illegally moved money between budgets, so called "pedaladas fiscais," or fiscal maneuvering. Rousseff and supporters said impeachment was a sham with the goal of removing a democratically elected president from office.

VICE PRESIDENT MICHEL TEMER: A backroom wheeler-dealer with enormous influence among members of Congress, Temer took over as president when Rousseff was impeached and eventually removed. Rousseff accused Temer of betraying her and having a lead role in the effort to oust her. Temer always denied this, arguing that he was simply fulfilling his constitutional duty to take over in the case the president could no longer do the job. Temer would finish Rousseff's second term, which ended Dec. 31, 2018. Since leaving office, Temer has been arrested twice (and released) on corruption charges and continues to fight cases against him in the courts.

HOUSE SPEAKER EDUARDO CUNHA: As leader of the Chamber of Deputies, Cunha submitted impeachment legislation against Rousseff in late 2015 and led the effort to remove her the following year. While Rousseff's popularity had tanked, and many Brazilians wanted her out of power, Cunha wasn't simply following popular will. He and Rousseff had a fraught relationship going back many years, allegations of corruption against Cunha were mounting and Rousseff had refused to lend her influence and help him prevail in a vote by the Chamber of Deputies ethics committee on whether he should be investigated and, if found guilty, stripped of his seat. Not long after guiding impeachment through the lower house, Cunha was stripped of his seat. He was later convicted and jailed for corruption. In May 2021, he was released from house arrest while he appeals his conviction.

SEN. AÉCIO NEVES: After losing the presidential election against Rousseff in 2014, Neves was a constant and vocal proponent of removing her in any way possible. While he was being investigated for corruption, Neves would point out corruption by members of the Workers' Party as one reason that Rousseff should go. He also argued the Rousseff-Temer ticket should be annulled because of alleged campaign finance violations and, when that effort didn't look to be producing fruit, he became a big proponent of impeachment.

JUDGE SERGIO MORO: A federal judge from the southeastern state of Paraná, Moro was a central figure in the Car Wash investigation, which uncovered a massive kickback scheme involving the nation's largest construction firms. He was both deified as an anti-corruption crusader and vilified as a judge willing to use controversial methods to get results. Moro and the Car Wash investigation had an enormous influence on the impeachment process even though Rousseff was not accused of corruption. Brazil's top court ruled in 2021 that Moro was biased against Lula, and his convictions against the former president were thrown out. The same court has also decided that Lula's cases should not have been tried in Moro's jurisdiction in Curitiba.

EX-PRESIDENT LUIZ INÁCIO LULA DA SILVA: President between 2003 and 2010, Lula left office with approval ratings nearing 90 percent. That popularity essentially allowed him to pick his replacement. He went with his chief of staff, Dilma Rousseff, despite the reality that she had never held public office. While Lula tried to help Rousseff during the impeachment process, his mounting legal woes, and by extension those of the Workers' Party, also weighed her down. In 2017, Lula was convicted of corruption and in 2018 began serving a sentence of just over 12 years. In 2021, the Supreme Federal Tribunal annulled the case on the grounds that it was tried in the wrong jurisdiction.

SOLICITOR GENERAL JOSÉ EDUARDO CARDOZO: A close Rousseff ally, Cardozo led the president's legal defense throughout the impeachment saga. Before becoming solicitor general, he had been justice minister. At every turn during impeachment, Cardozo argued that Rousseff had not committed "crimes of responsibility," and that the fiscal management infractions she was accused of were legal and employed by previous presidents. Cardozo also made many appeals to the Supreme Federal Tribunal to stop the proceedings.

CONGRESSMAN JAIR BOLSONARO: A former army captain turned politician, Bolsonaro gained notoriety for provocative statements that were sometimes racist, homophobic and sexist. While accomplishing very little legislatively during nearly three decades in Congress, Bolsonaro was an outspoken critic of the Workers' Party and left-leaning governments in general. Speaking with nostalgia about the 1964-1985 dictatorship, Bolsonaro would argue that Brazil had lost its way and could only return to a good path by cracking down on corruption, rooting out dangerous leftist movements and returning to "traditional values." Bolsonaro was elected president in 2018 and took over on Jan. 1, 2019. In the years since taking office, his popularity has dropped sharply amid his handling of the coronavirus pandemic and his administration's failure to stimulate economic growth.

SEN. DELCÍDIO DO AMARAL: An engineer turned senator from the state of Mato Grosso do Sul, Amaral was Petrobras director during the presidency of Fernando Henrique Cardoso in the 1990s. Joining the Workers' Party, Amaral became a household name after chairing an investigation into alleged kickbacks for votes in Congress during the Lula administration in 2005. He rose in the Workers' Party ranks after Rousseff became president in 2011, eventually becoming whip in the Senate. Imprisonment in 2015 and a plea bargain deal led to him losing his seat in the Senate and being suspended from the Workers' Party.

CHIEF JUSTICE RICARDO LEWANDOWSKI: Appointed by Lula, Lewandowski would preside over Rousseff's impeachment trial in the Senate and reportedly took part in discussions to separate the vote for removal from the decision on her political rights. He was a critic of the methods of the Car Wash probe from the start. On many occasions, he ruled in line with the opinions of leaders of the Workers' Party, which made him a target of far-right critics on social media.

SEN. RENAN CALHEIROS: An ally of every president except Bolsonaro since Brazil's redemocratization in the 1980s, Calheiros started his career in the 1970s in local politics, then was elected to the Chamber of Deputies. He became a senator for the state of Alagoas in 1994. Calheiros has kept that seat despite a series of corruption scandals. Having developed a working relationship with Rousseff over the years, Calheiros initially opposed impeachment and reportedly helped orchestrate the effort to allow Rousseff to keep her political rights after being ousted from the presidency.

WORKERS' PARTY: Lula's and Rousseff's party was founded in 1980 with the support of leftist union leaders and intellectuals. It was one of the main parties leading Brazil's return to democracy. The party started gaining traction after electing its first mayor of a major city in 1985, Maria Luíza Fontenele in Fortaleza. Three consecutive defeats in presidential elections, however, started moving the party to the center. The PT, the party's acronym in Portuguese, only elected a big number of lawmakers and governors after Lula was elected president in 2002 with a business leader as his running mate. Since Rousseff was removed and Lula's legal problems began, the party has struggled to produce new leaders. One of those willing to carry the party forward, former São Paulo Mayor Fernando Haddad, lost the 2018 presidential elections to Jair Bolsonaro.

BRAZILIAN DEMOCRATIC MOVEMENT PARTY: Many Brazilians see today's PMDB (it's name was tweaked to Brazilan Democratic Movement, or MDB, in 2017) as a symbol of moderation plus corruption, with a reputation for allegiance to any president who is good for the party. But it was very different in December 1965, when it was founded as the only party for all adversaries of the country's military dictatorship. Leftists, social democrats, liberals and even some conservatives were part of its ranks until 1979, when a political reopening process began allowing the creation of new parties. Brazil's military rule was set to end in a congressional election for president in 1985, with PMDB's Tancredo Neves as favorite and a former ally of the regime, José Sarney, as his running mate. Neves won, but died of diverticulitis before he took office. Since democracy was restored in the late 1980s, the PMDB, which is often the party with most elected mayors and lawmakers, has failed to come up with a competitive national candidate. Instead, the party has traditionally had a kingmaker role. That helped party leader Michel Temer be chosen as Rousseff's running mate in 2010 and 2014.

BRAZILIAN SOCIAL DEMOCRACY PARTY: The PSDB was founded in 1988 with social democratic business leaders, intellectuals and some traditional politicians who believed they did not fit into the moderate

PMDB. The party organized quickly and allowed former São Paulo Mayor Mario Covas to finish the 1989 presidential race in fourth place. Five years later, the "toucans," as PSDB members are called, catapulted former Economy Minister Fernando Henrique Cardoso to the presidency, on the back of his role in the creation of a new currency that stemmed inflation. After Cardoso left office in 2003, the PSDB was the Workers' Party main adversary in Congress and in presidential elections. Since Rousseff's impeachment and its role in the Temer administration, the PSDB has lost ground nationally to other forces.

ODEBRECHT: Founded in the 1940s, Odebrecht grew into one of Brazil's most powerful construction companies, with national influence that went far beyond the mega projects it undertook. Not only did it invest heavily in political campaigns, but the company's bribing of politicians and other officials was widely known. Then-CEO Emilio Odebrecht acknowledged bribes in the early 1990s. However, the Car Wash investigation into kickbacks to politicians — bribes financed by inflated construction contracts — would uncover a graft scheme shocking even in a country that has long struggled with endemic corruption. Odebrecht was a central player in the scandal emanating from state oil company Petrobras, and fallout from the investigation would lead to the arrest and jailing of many of the country's elite, including CEO Marcelo Odebrecht and many top members of the Workers' Party and other parties.

Books Cited or Reviewed

Amaral, Ricardo Batista. *A vida quer é a coragem — A trajetória de Dilma Rousseff, a primeira presidenta do Brasil*. Rio de Janeiro: Sextante, 2011. Print.

Campos, Pedro Henrique Pedreira. *ESTRANHAS CATEDRAIS — As empreiteiras brasileiras e a ditadura civil-militar, 1964-1985*. Niterói, Brazil: Eduff, 2014. Print

Conti, Mário Sérgio. *Notícias do Planalto: A imprensa e o poder nos anos Collor*. São Paulo: Companhia das Letras, 2012. Print

Cunha, Eduardo. *TCHAU, QUERIDA — O Diário do Impeachment*. São Paulo: Matrix, 2021. Print

De Almeida, Rodrigo. *À Sombra do Poder: Bastidores da Crise que Derrubou Dilma Rousseff*. São Paulo: LeYa Brasil, 2016. Print.

Foundation, Ulysses Guimarães. *50 ANOS PMDB, O PARTIDO QUE MUDA O BRASIL*. Brasília: Editora Positiva, 2016. Print.

Franco, Bernardo Mello. *Mil Dias de Tormenta: A crise que derrubou Dilma e deixou Temer por um fio*. São Paulo: Editora Objetiva, 2018. Print

Gonçalves, Leandro Pereira and Odilon Caldeira Neto. *O Fascismo em Camisas Verdes*. Rio de Janeiro: Editora FGV, 2020. Print

Green, James. *We Cannot Remain Silent: Opposition to the Brazilian Military Dictatorship in the United States (Radical Perspectives)*. Durham: Duke University Press Books, 2010. Print

Books Cited or Reviewed

Levitsky, Steven and Daniel Ziblatt. *How Democracies Die*. New York: Crown, 2018. Print

Netto, Vladimir. *Lava Jato — O juiz Sergio Moro e os bastidores da operação que abalou o Brasil*. Rio de Janeiro: Sextante, 2016. Print

Temer, Michel. *MICHEL TEMER A ESCOLHA: Como um Presidente Conseguiu Superar Grave Crise e Apresentar uma Agenda Para o Brasil*. São Paulo: Noeses, 2020. Print.

Traumann, Thomas. *O Pior Emprego do Mundo: 14 ministros da fazenda contam como tomaram as decisões que mudaram o Brasil e mexeram no seu bolso*. São Paulo: Editora Planeta do Brasil, 2018. Print

Recondo, Felipe and Luiz Weber. *Os Onze: o STF, seus bastidores e suas crises*. São Paulo: Companhia das Letras, 2019. Print

Schwartz, Lilia Mortiz and Heloisa M. Starling. *Brazil (A Biography)*. New York: Farrar, Straus and Giroux, 2018. Print

Secco, Lincoln. *História do PT*. São Paulo: Ateliê Editorial, 2018. Print.

Singer, André. *O lulismo em crise: um quebra-cabeça do período Dilma (2011-2016)*. São Paulo: Companhia das Letras, 2018. Print

Other Academic Works
Cited or Reviewed

Carniel, Fagner, Lennita Ruggi and Júlia de Oliveira Ruggi. *Gênero e humor nas redes sociais: a campanha contra Dilma Rousseff no Brasil*. Campinas, Brazil: Opinião Pública, 2018. Online.

Chalhoub, Sidney, Cath Collins, Mariana Llanos, Mónica Pachón and Keisha-Khan Y. Perry. *Report of the LASA fact-finding delegation on the impeachment of Brazilian President Dilma Rousseff*. Pittsburgh, PA: Latin American Studies Association, 2017. Online.

Mora, Mônica. *A Evolução do Crédito no Brasil entre 2003 e 2010*. Rio de Janeiro: Instituto de Pesquisa Econômica Aplicada, 2015. Online.

Moro, Sergio Fernando. *CONSIDERAÇÕES SOBRE A OPERAÇÃO MANI PULITE*. São Paulo: Consultor Jurídico, 2004. Online.

Photo Credits

Chapter 1
(AP Photo/Eraldo Peres)

Chapter 2
(AP Photo/Eraldo Peres)

Chapter 3
(AP Photo/Eraldo Peres)

Chapter 4
(AP Photo/Eraldo Peres)

Chapter 5
(AP Photo/Leo Correa)

Chapter 6
(AP Photo/Andre Penner)

Chapter 7
(AP Photo/Eraldo Peres)

Chapter 8
(AP Photo/Andre Penner)

Chapter 9
(AP Photo/Cassiano Rosario/Futura Press via AP)

Chapter 10
(AP Photo/Andre Penner)

Chapter 11
(AP Photo/Andre Penner)

Chapter 12
(AP Photo/Eraldo Peres)

Chapter 13
(AP Photo/Andre Penner)

Chapter 14
(AP Photo/Eraldo Peres)

Chapter 15
(AP Photo/Eraldo Peres)

Chapter 16
(AP Photo/Leo Correa)

Chapter 17
(AP Photo/Felipe Dana)

Chapter 18
(AP Photo/Andre Penner)

Chapter 19
(AP Photo/Jae C. Hong)

Chapter 20
(AP Photo/Eraldo Peres)

Chapter 21
(AP Photo/Leo Correa)

About the Authors

 **Peter Prengaman** has been with The Associated Press since 2002. He has covered major stories in more than 15 countries and held several positions in many locations, from statehouse reporter in Oregon to Brazil bureau chief. He is currently the AP's news director for the Western U.S., overseeing all editorial operations in 13 states. Prengaman lives in Phoenix with his wife and three sons.

 **Mauricio Savarese** has covered politics, the economy and sports for several media outlets since 2004. In 2015, Savarese joined the AP and has covered everything from the 2018 World Cup in Russia to indigenous tribes in the Amazon. He is co-author of *A to Zico: An Alphabet of Brazilian Football*. Savarese lives in São Paulo with his partner and daughter.

Former President Dilma Rousseff is interviewed by AP's Mauricio Savarese in her apartment's library, January 22, 2017. (Courtesy Mauricio Savarese)

CPSIA information can be obtained
at www.ICGtesting.com
Printed in the USA
JSHW030927131021
19486JS00008B/18